MW01590882

KURT COBAIN

Biography

Rock tunes and bumpy life

Gabriel Jose Ramirez

Copyright © 2023
All rights reserved

The content of this book may not be reproduced, duplicated, or transmitted without the author's or publisher's express written permission. Under no circumstances will the publisher or author be held liable or legally responsible for any damages, reparation, or monetary loss caused by the information contained in this book, whether directly or indirectly.

Legal Notice:
This publication is copyrighted. It is strictly for personal use only. You may not change, distribute, sell, use, quote, or paraphrase any part of this book without the author's or publisher's permission.

Disclaimer Notice:
Please keep in mind that the information in this document is only for educational and entertainment purposes. Every effort has been made to present accurate, up-to-date, reliable, and comprehensive information. There are no express or implied warranties. Readers understand that the author is not providing legal, financial, medical, or professional advice. This book's content was compiled from a variety of sources. Please seek the advice of a licensed professional before attempting any of the techniques described in this book. By reading this document, the reader agrees that the author is not liable for any direct or indirect losses incurred as a result of using the information contained within this document, including, but not limited to, errors, omissions, or inaccuracies.

TABLE OF CONTENTS

1:

Yelling Loudly at First

Kurt Donald Cobain was born in a hospital on a hill overlooking Aberdeen, Washington on February 20, 1967. Kurt's parents lived in nearby Hoquiam, but it was fitting that he was born in Aberdeen-he would spend three-quarters of his life within 10 miles of the hospital and would be forever emotionally attached to this landscape.

Anyone looking out the window of Grays Harbor Community Hospital on that wet Monday would have seen a place of harsh beauty, where forests, mountains, rivers, and a powerful ocean met in a spectacular vista. The junction of three rivers that ran into the adjacent Pacific Ocean was bordered by tree-covered hills. Aberdeen, Grays Harbor County's largest city, with a population of 19,000, was at the epicentre of it all. Kurt's parents, Don and Wendy, lived in a tiny cottage in Hoquiam, which was immediately to the west. And across the Chehalis River, to the south, was Cosmopolis, home of his mother's family, the Fradenburgs. On a clear day, which was rare in a region that received more than 80 inches of rain each year, one could see the nine miles to Montesano, where Kurt's grandfather Leland Cobain grew up. Kurt would eventually become Aberdeen's most famous product in such a small world with so few degrees of separation.

The vista from the three-story hospital was dominated by the West Coast's sixth busiest working harbour. There were so many pieces of timber floating in the Chehalis that you could walk across the two-mile mouth with them. Aberdeen's downtown was to the east, where retailers complained that the incessant rumble of logging trucks scared away customers. It was a metropolis at work, and the effort was nearly exclusively based on commercialising Douglas fir trees from the neighbouring hills. Aberdeen had 37 separate timber, pulp, shingle, or saw mills, and their smokestacks overshadowed the town's highest structure, which was only seven floors tall. Directly down the hill from the hospital was the massive Rayonier Mill smokestack, the tallest of all, stretching 150 feet toward the skies and spewing an endless heavenly cloud of wood-pulp effluence.

Despite the fact that Aberdeen was buzzing with activity around the time of Kurt's birth, the city's economy was slowly declining. The county was one of the few in the state with a shrinking population as unemployed people moved elsewhere. The timber industry was starting to feel the effects of offshore competition and over-logging. There were tracts of clear-cut trees outside of town, now only a memory of early settlers who "tried to cut it all," as the title of a local history book put it. Unemployment exacted a more sinister social cost on the community in the form of rising drunkenness, domestic violence, and suicide. In 1967, there were 27 bars, and the downtown core had several abandoned buildings, some of which had been brothels before they were closed in the late 1950s. The city was so notorious for whorehouses that Look magazine described it in 1952 as "one of the hot spots in America's battle against sin."

Despite the urban squalor of downtown Aberdeen, a close-knit social society existed where neighbours aided neighbours, parents were interested in schools, and family ties remained strong amid a diverse immigrant population. Churches outnumbered pubs, and it was a location where, like most of small-town America in the mid-1960s, youngsters on bikes were allowed to roam freely. As he grew older, the entire city would become Kurt's backyard.

Kurt's birth, like most firsts, was a joyous occasion for both his parents and the rest of the family. On his mother's side, he had six aunts and uncles; on his father's side, he had two uncles; and he was the first grandchild for both family branches. These were vast families, and when his mother went to make birth announcements, she went through 50 before she finished with the immediate relatives. Kurt's birth was announced in the Aberdeen Daily World's birth column on February 23: "To Mr. and Mrs. Donald Cobain, 283012 Aberdeen Avenue, Hoquiam, February 20, at Community Hospital, a son."

Kurt weighed seven pounds, seven and a half ounces at birth, and he had black hair and skin. His newborn hair would turn blond and his pigmentation would lighten after five months. Kurt acquired his pointy chin from his father's side, whose family had come from Skey Townland in County Tyrone, Ireland, in 1875. Kurt inherited pink cheeks and blond hair from his mother's side Fradenburgh, who were German, Irish, and English. His amazing azure eyes, however, were by far his most outstanding feature; even nurses in the hospital exclaimed on their attractiveness.

Aberdeen felt more like 1950s America than 1960s America, despite the fact that a war was raging in Vietnam. The Aberdeen Daily World juxtaposed the great news of an American triumph at Quang Ngai City with local reporting on the extent of the timber harvest and ads from JCPenney, where a Washington's Birthday sale featured $2.48 flannel shirts on the day Kurt was born. Who Is Fearful of Virginia Woolf? In Los Angeles that afternoon, it had gotten thirteen Academy Award nominations, but the Aberdeen drive-in was showing Girls on the Beach.

Kurt's 21-year-old father, Don, worked as a mechanic at the Chevron station in Hoquiam. Don was attractive and athletic, but his flat top hairdo and Buddy Holly-style spectacles gave him a geeky appearance. Wendy, Kurt's 19-year-old mother, was a classic beauty who looked and dressed like Marcia Brady. Wendy, who acquired the nickname "Breeze" in high school, had fallen pregnant the previous June, only weeks after her high school graduation. Don took his father's sedan and made up an excuse to drive to Idaho and married without parental permission.

Kurt was born while the young couple was living in a little house in the backyard of another house in Hoquiam. Wendy looked after the infant while Don worked long hours at the service station. Kurt slept in a white wicker bassinet adorned with a bright yellow ribbon. Money was tight, but a few weeks after the baby was born, they were able to save enough to move out of the tiny house and into a larger one at 2830 Aberdeen Avenue. "The rent," says Don, "was only an extra five dollars a month, but in those times, five dollars was a lot of money."

If there was a sign of trouble in the house, it was over money. Don had been made "lead man" at Chevron in early 1968, but his annual compensation was barely $6,000 USD. Most of their neighbours and acquaintances worked in the forestry business, where employment was physically demanding-one study called it "more deadly than war"-but paid well. The Cobains battled to keep costs down, but when it came to Kurt, they made sure he was well-dressed and even paid for professional shots. Kurt appears in a sequence of photos from this era sporting a white dress shirt, a black tie, and a grey suit, looking like Little Lord Fauntleroy-he still has his baby fat and plump, full cheeks. In another, he's dressed in a matching blue vest and suit top, as well as a hat fit for Phillip Marlowe rather than a year-and-a-half-old boy.

Wendy's fourteen-year-old sister Mari submitted a paper about her nephew for her home economics class in May 1968, when Kurt was fifteen months old. "His mother takes care of him most of the time," she wrote. "[She] expresses her love for him by holding him, giving him praise when he deserves it, and participating in many of his activities." He responds to his father in that he smiles when he sees him and enjoys having his father hold him. Mari recorded that his favourite game was peekaboo, that his first tooth appeared at eight months, and that his first dozen words were, "coco, momma, dadda, ball, toast, bye-bye, hi, baby, me, love, hot dog, and kittie."

Mari mentioned a harp, a drum, a basketball, vehicles, trucks, blocks, a pounding block, a toy TV, and a telephone as his favourite toys. She stated of Kurt's daily routine, "his reaction to sleep is that he cries when he is laid down to do so." "He is so interested in the family that he doesn't want to leave them," his aunt said.

Wendy was a thoughtful mother, reading learning books, purchasing flash cards, and ensuring Kurt received good care with the help of her brothers and sisters. Kurt thrived in the spotlight as the entire extended family celebrated the birth of this youngster. "I can't even put into words the joy and the life that Kurt brought into our family," Mari said. "He was this small human being that was always smiling. Even as a baby, he exuded charm. Kurt was clever enough that when his aunt couldn't figure out how to lower his crib, the one-and-a-half-year-old simply did it himself. Wendy was so taken with her son's antics that she leased a Super-8 camera and began filming him-an cost the family couldn't afford. In one video, a cheerful, smiling little boy cuts his second-year birthday cake and appears to be the centre of his parents' universe.

Kurt was already interested in music by his second Christmas. Wendy's older brother Chuck was in a band called the Beachcombers; Mari played guitar; her great-uncle Delbert had a career as an Irish tenor, featured in the film The King of Jazz. Kurt was captivated by the family jam sessions when the Cobains visited Cosmopolis. His aunts and uncles taped him performing the Beatles' "Hey Jude," Arlo Guthrie's "Motorcycle Song," and the theme to "The Monkees" television show. Even as a toddler, Kurt enjoyed making up his own lyrics. When he was four, he sat down at the piano after returning from a trip to the park with Mari and composed a crude song about their excursion. "We went to the park, and we got candy," the song continued. "I was just amazed," Mari recounted. "I should have plugged in the tape recorder-it was probably his first song."

Kurt made an imaginary companion named Boddah not long after he turned two. Kurt's parents were concerned about his commitment to this phantom companion, so when an uncle was deployed to Vietnam, he was informed that Boddah had also been enlisted. Kurt, on the other hand, was sceptical. Kurt was three years old when he was playing with his aunt's tape machine, which had been set to "echo." When he heard the echo, he wondered, "Is that voice talking to me?" Boddah? Boddah?"

Don and Wendy purchased their first home in Aberdeen, 1210 East First Street, in September 1969, when Kurt was two and a half years old. The house had two stories, 1,000 square feet, with a yard and a garage. It cost them $7,950. The 1923-era house was in a neighbourhood known as "felony flats." To the north was the Wishkah River, which frequently flooded, and to the southeast was the wooded bluff known as "Think of Me Hill"-at the turn of the century, it featured an advertisement for Think of Me cigars.

The property was in a middle-class area, which Kurt subsequently described as "white trash posing as middle-class." The first floor had the living room, dining room, kitchen, and Wendy and Don's bedroom. The second floor contained three rooms: a tiny playroom and two bedrooms, one of which became Kurt's. The other was for Kurt's sibling; Wendy had found out she was expecting again that month.

Kurt was three years old when his sister Kimberly arrived. Even as an infant, she resembled her brother, with the same captivating blue eyes and light blond hair. Kurt insisted on carrying Kimberly inside the house after she was brought home from the hospital. "He loved her so much," his father recalled. "And at first, they were darling together." Their three-year age gap was great since her care became one of his main topics of conversation. This was the beginning of a personality trait that would follow Kurt for the rest of his life: he was extremely sensitive to the wants and pains of others.

Having two children affected the dynamic of the Cobain household, and what little free time they had was spent on family visits or Don's interest in intramural sports. Don played basketball in the winter and baseball in the summer, and much of their social life revolved around going to games or post-game events. Rod and Dres Herling met and befriended the Cobains through athletics. "They were good family people, and they did lots of things with their kids," Rod Herling said. They were also unusually square in comparison to other Americans in the 1960s: no one in their social circle smoked marijuana at the time, and Don and Wendy rarely drank.

The Herlings were playing cards with the Cobain's one summer evening when Don rushed into the living room and proclaimed, "I have a rat." Rats were widespread in Aberdeen due to the low elevation and quantity of water. Don started making a rudimentary spear out of a butcher knife and a broom handle. Kurt, a five-year-old boy, was intrigued and followed his father to the garage, where the rat was hiding in a garbage can. Don told Kurt to back up, but with such a curious child, the boy inched closer and closer until he was grasping his father's pant leg. Rod Herling was supposed to lift the can's lid, after which Don would stab the rat with his spear. Don hurled the broomstick but missed the rat, and Herling lifted, and the spear caught on the floor. As Don struggled to take the broom out, the rat crept up the broomstick, jumped over Don's shoulder and down to the ground, and ran over Kurt's foot as he departed the garage. It happened in an instant, but the combination of Don's expression and the size of Kurt's eyes made everyone howl with laughter. They laughed for hours over this incident, which became family lore: "Hey, remember that time Dad tried to spear the rat?""No one laughed harder than Kurt, but he laughed at everything as a five-year-old." It was a lovely chuckle, like a baby being tickled, and it was a constant refrain.

Kurt started kindergarten at Robert Gray Elementary, three streets north of his house, in September 1972. Wendy drove him to school the first day, but he was on his own after that; the neighbourhood around First Street had become his domain. His teachers recognized him as a bright, curious student with a Snoopy lunchbox. His teacher noted "really good student" on his report card that year because he was not shy. Kurt was one of the only kids who posed for photos with a bear cub when it was brought in for show-and-tell.

The subject in which he excelled the most was art. At the age of five, it was evident he possessed outstanding artistic abilities: he was producing paintings that appeared realistic. Tony Hirschman met Kurt in kindergarten and was blown away by his ability: "He could draw anything." We were looking at images of werewolves one time, and he drew one that looked exactly like the photo." Kurt painted a series that year that featured Aqua-man, the Creature From the Black Lagoon, Mickey Mouse, and Pluto. Every holiday and birthday, his family would give him supplies, and his room began to resemble an art studio.

Iris Cobain, Kurt's paternal grandmother, pushed him to pursue his artistic interests. She was a Norman Rockwell fan who collected Franklin Mint plates with Saturday Evening Post illustrations on them. She needlepointed many of Rockwell's motifs, and his most renowned painting, "Freedom From Want," depicting the traditional American Thanksgiving table, sat on the wall of her Montesano doublewide trailer. Iris even persuaded Kurt to assist her in a favourite hobby: carving rough replicas of Norman Rockwell's artwork onto the tops of freshly harvested fungus with toothpicks. When these colossal mushrooms dried, the toothpick scratchings remained, like backwoods scrimshaw.

Leland Cobain, Iris's husband and Kurt's grandfather, wasn't artistic-he had driven an asphalt roller, which had cost him much of his hearing-but he did teach Kurt woodworking. Leland was a harsh and crusty figure, and when his grandson showed off a drawing of

Mickey Mouse he'd done (Kurt was a big Disney fan), Leland accused him of tracing it. "I did not," Kurt said. "You did, too," Leland said. Leland handed Kurt a new piece of paper and a pencil, saying, "Here, draw me another one and show me how you did it." The six-year-old went down and drew a near-perfect drawing of Donald Duck and another of Goofy without a model. He looked up from the paper with a wide grin, as thrilled as he was to show off his grandfather as he was to create his favourite duck.

His inventiveness grew to include music. He never had formal piano lessons, yet he could play a basic melody by ear. "Even when he was a little kid," his sister Kim said, "he could sit down and just play something he'd heard on the radio." Don and Wendy got Kurt a Mickey Mouse drum kit, which he passionately beat every day after school, to encourage him. Though he liked the plastic drums, he preferred the actual drums at Uncle Chuck's place since they allowed him to create more noise. He also liked strapping on Aunt Mari's guitar, despite the fact that it was so heavy that it made his knees buckle. He'd strum it while making up songs. That same year, he purchased his first album, a sugary single by Terry Jacks titled "Seasons in the Sun."

He also enjoyed perusing his aunts' and uncles' photo albums. When he was six, he went to see Aunt Mari and was looking through her record collection for a Beatles album-they were one of his favourites. Kurt screamed angrily and dashed for his aunt. He was holding a copy of the Beatles' Yesterday and Today, which had the iconic "Butcher cover," which depicted the band with meat on their faces. "It made me realise how impressionable he was at that age," Mari said.

He was also aware of the growing tension between his parents. There hadn't been any conflict in the home for the first few years of Kurt's life, but there had also been little evidence of a major love affair. Don and Wendy, like many young married couples, were overwhelmed by circumstance. Their children were the centre of their lives, and the little passion they'd had previous to having children was difficult to revive. Don was overwhelmed by financial difficulties, while Wendy was consumed by caring for two children. They started arguing and yelling at each other in front of the kids. "You have no idea how hard I work," Don yelled at Wendy, who agreed with her husband.

Nonetheless, Kurt's upbringing was filled with joy. They'd spend the summer in a Fradenburg family cabin on Washaway Beach on the Washington coast. They used to go sledding in the winter. They would drive east into the little hills past the logging hamlet of Porter and to Fuzzy Top Mountain because it rarely snowed in Aberdeen. They'd park, bring out a toboggan for Don and Wendy, a silver saucer for Kim, and Kurt's Flexible Flyer, and ready to slide down the hill. Kurt would grab his sled, take off running, and hurl himself down the slope like an athlete would begin the long jump. When he reached the bottom, he would wave to his parents, signalling that he had survived the journey. The rest of the family would join them as they walked back up the hill. They'd go through the motions for hours, until darkness fell or Kurt collapsed from tiredness. Kurt would make them vow to return the next weekend as they walked toward the car. Kurt will later recall these events as his favourite childhood recollections.

Kurt was six years old when his family went to a downtown picture studio for a formal Christmas shot. Wendy is seated in the centre of the frame, with a spotlight above her head producing a halo; she is wearing a long white-and-pink-striped Victorian gown with ruffled cuffs and is wearing an oversized, wooden high-backed chair. Her shoulder-length strawberry blond hair is parted in the centre, with not a single strand out of place, and she wears a black necklace around her neck. She appears to be a queen, with her flawless posture and the way her wrists droop over the armrests of the chair.

Kim, three, sits on her mother's lap. She appears to be a little version of her mother, dressed in a long white gown and black patent leather shoes. She is staring directly at the camera and has the expression of a child who could cry at any time.

Don stands behind the chair, close enough to be in the shot but far enough away to be distracted. His shoulders are somewhat hunched, and he sports a puzzled expression rather than a genuine smile. He's dressed in a light purple long-sleeved shirt with a four-inch collar and a grey vest, the kind of outfit Steve Martin or Dan Aykroyd might wear for their "wild and crazy guys" skit on "Saturday Night Live." He has a distant look in his eyes, as if he's wondering why he's been dragged down to the photo studio when he could be playing ball.

Kurt is standing to the left of his father, a foot or two away from the chair. He's dressed in two-tone, striped blue slacks, a matching vest, and a fire-truck red long-sleeved shirt that's a little too big for him, the sleeves covering his hands somewhat. He is not only smiling, but also laughing as the family's actual entertainment. He seemed to be having a good time with his family on a Saturday.

The external appearances suggest an all-American pedigree-clean hair, bright teeth, and well-pressed clothes so styled they could have been taken from an early seventies Sears catalogue. A closer look exposes a dynamic that must have been painfully clear even to the photographer: it's a picture of a family, not a portrait of a marriage. Don and Wendy aren't touching, and there's no sign of affection between them; it's as if they're not even in the same frame of mind. With Kurt in front of Don and Kim on Wendy's lap, a pair of scissors might easily slice the photograph-and the family-down the middle. You'd be left with two distinct families, each with one adult and one child, each with a distinct gender-the Victorian clothes on one side and the boys with wide collars on the other.

2:

I Hate Mom, I Hate Dad

When Don Cobain chose to change careers and work in the timber sector in 1974, the family's stress level rose. Don wasn't a big guy, and he didn't want to be cutting down 200-foot trees, so he worked in the office at Mayr Brothers. He knew he could make more money in lumber than he did at the service station, but his first position was entry-level, paying $4.10 an hour, which was even less than he'd made as a mechanic. He supplemented his income by doing inventory at the mill on weekends, and he frequently brought Kurt with him. "He'd ride his little bike around the yard," Don said. Kurt would later disparage his father's career, claiming that accompanying Don to work was misery, but at the time he thrived in being included. Though he spent his entire adult life attempting to convince himself differently, Kurt valued his father's acknowledgement and attention, and he desired more of it, not less. He would subsequently concede that his childhood memories of his nuclear family were happy ones. "I had a really good childhood," he said in Spin magazine in 1992, but only "up until I was nine."

Don and Wendy frequently had to borrow money to pay their expenses, which was a major source of contention between them. Leland and Iris kept $20 cash in their kitchen, joking that it was a bouncing twenty since they'd loan it to their son for groceries each month, and then quickly repay it, and Don would borrow it again. "He'd go around, pay all his bills, and then come to our house," Leland recalled. "He'd give us our $20 and then say, 'Hell, I did pretty well this week.'" "Leland, who never liked Wendy because he thought she acted "better than the Cobains," remembers the young family going to the Blue Beacon Drive-In on Boone Street to spend the change on hamburgers. Though Don got along well with his father-in-law, Charles Fradenburg, who operated a county road grader, Leland and Wendy never clicked.

Tensions between the two erupted when Leland assisted with the renovation of the house on First Street. He constructed Don and Wendy a faux fireplace in the living room and installed new countertops, but he and Wendy fought often. Leland ultimately informed his son that if Wendy didn't stop bothering him, he'd quit and leave the project unfinished. "It was the first time I ever heard Donnie talk back to her," Leland said. "She was bitching about this and that, and finally he said, 'Keep your goddamn mouth shut or he'll take his tools and go home.' And she shut her mouth for once."

Don, like his father before him, was severe with his children. Wendy complained that her husband wanted the kids to constantly behave— an unattainable standard—and required Kurt to act like a "little adult." Kurt, like many children, was a terror at times. At the time, most of his acting-out instances were minor—he'd draw on the walls, slam the door, or torment his sister. These actions frequently resulted in a spanking, but Don's more common—and nearly daily—physical punishment was to hit Kurt on the temple or chest with two fingers. It barely wounded a bit, but the psychological impact was severe—it made his kid fear more physical harm and reinforced Don's power. Kurt began to withdraw into his room's closet. He found safety in the kinds of restricted, constricted situations that would give others panic attacks.

And there were other things to keep hidden: both parents might be snarky and insulting. When Kurt was young enough to believe them, Don and Wendy warned him that if he wasn't good, he'd get a lump of coal for Christmas, especially if he argued with his sister. They left bits of coal in his stocking as a joke. "It was just a joke," Don recalls. "Every year, we did it." He got presents and everything—we never didn't give him stuff." The irony, however, eluded Kurt, at least as he remembered the incident later in life. He claimed that one year he was promised a Starsky and Hutch toy gun, which never arrived. Instead, he claimed he merely received a beautifully wrapped lump of coal. Kurt's story was exaggerated, but he had begun to put his own spin on the family in his mind.

Kim and Kurt would occasionally get along and play together. Though Kim lacked Kurt's artistic skills and was always jealous of how much attention the rest of the family lavished on him, she acquired a gift for impersonating voices. She was especially brilliant at Mickey Mouse and Donald Duck, which made Kurt very happy. Wendy's voice powers even gave birth to a new fantasy. "It was my mom's big dream," Kim told me, "that Kurt and I would end up at Disneyland, both of us working there, with him drawing and me doing voices."

Kurt was eight years old in March 1975, and he was overjoyed because he had finally visited Disneyland and had taken his first aeroplane ride. Leland retired in 1974, and he and Iris spent the winter in Arizona that year. Don and Wendy took Kurt to Seattle, where he boarded a plane, and Leland met him in Yuma before they flew to Southern California. They went to Disneyland, Knotts Berry Farm, and Universal Studios in two days. Kurt was captivated and insisted on riding the "Pirates of the Caribbean" ride three times. He rode the enormous roller coaster at Knotts Berry Farm, but when he got off, his face was as white as a ghost. "Had enough?" said Leland." The colour returned, and he rode the coaster once more. Kurt leaned out of the train in front of the Jaws shark during his Universal Studios tour, prompting a guard to yell at his grandparents, "You better pull that little towheaded boy back or his head will get bitten off." Kurt defied the order and snapped a picture of the shark's mouth as it came inches away from his camera. Later that day, while driving on the interstate, Kurt fell asleep in the backseat, which was the only way his grandparents could sneak by Magic Mountain without him insisting.

Kurt was the most close to his grandmother Iris, with whom he shared a love in art and, at times, grief. "They adored each other," Kim recalled. "I think he intuitively knew the hell she'd been through." Both Iris and Leland had traumatic upbringings, damaged by poverty and the deaths of their fathers on the job when they were young. Iris' father was killed by hazardous vapours in the Rayonier Pulp Mill, and Leland's father perished when his revolver accidentally discharged. Leland was fifteen years old when his father died. He joined the Marines and was deployed to Guadalcanal, but after assaulting an officer, he was taken to a hospital for psychiatric treatment. After his discharge, he married Iris, but he suffered with alcohol and rage, especially after their third son, Michael, was born disabled and died in an institution at the age of six. "On Friday nights, he'd get paid and then come home drunk," Don recounted. "He used to hit my mother. He'd humiliate me. He beat my grandmother and Grandma's boyfriend. But that was the way it was back then." By Kurt's adolescence, Leland had softened, and his most lethal weapon was nasty words.

When Leland and Iris weren't available, one of the Fradenburg siblings—three of Kurt's aunts lived within four blocks—would babysit. Don's younger brother Gary was also assigned child-care duties on a few occasions, and one of these occasions marked Kurt's first return to the hospital. "I broke his right arm," Gary said. "I was on my back and he was on my feet, and I was shooting him up in the air with my feet." Kurt was a highly energetic child, and family were amazed he didn't break more limbs with all the running around he did.

Kurt's fractured arm healed, and he continued to participate in sports. Don encouraged his son to play baseball practically as soon as he could walk and equipped him with all of the necessary balls, bats, and mitts. Kurt found the bats more useful as percussion instruments as a toddler, but he gradually began to participate in athletics, first in the neighbourhood and subsequently in organised play. He was on his first Little League team when he was seven years old. The coach was his father. "He wasn't the best player on the team, but he wasn't bad," said Gary Cobain. "He didn't seem to want to play, mentally," I reasoned. "I believe he did it because of his father."

Baseball was an example of Kurt attempting to gain Don's approval. "Kurt and my dad got along well when he was young," Kim says, "but Kurt wasn't anything like how Dad was planning on Kurt turning out."

Don and Wendy were both dealing with the contradiction between the idealised child and the actual child. Kurt's birth brought out all of their own expectations because they both had unmet demands from their own childhoods. Don desired the father/son relationship he had never had with Leland, and he believed that playing sports together would give that closeness. And, while Kurt enjoyed athletics, especially when his father wasn't around, he intuitively linked his father's love for this pastime, something that would stick with him for the rest of his life. His instinct was to participate, but he did it reluctantly.

Kurt's parents and instructor decided his boundless energy had a greater medical cause while he was in second grade. Kurt was advised by his paediatrician, and Red Dye Number Two was eliminated from his diet. Kurt's sugar intake was restricted when there was no improvement. Finally, Kurt's doctor recommended Ritalin, which he took for three months. "He was a little hyperactive," Kim said. "He was bouncing off the walls, particularly if you got any sugar in him."

Other relatives believe Kurt had attention deficit hyperactivity disorder (ADHD). Mari recalled paying a visit to Kurt Cobain's residence and finding him rushing around the neighbourhood, banging on a marching drum and shrieking at the top of his lungs. Mari rushed inside and inquired of her sister, "What on earth is he doing?""I'm not sure,' ' Wendy replied. "I don't know what to do to get him to stop—I've tried everything." Wendy assumed it was Kurt's method of expanding his boyish energy at the moment.

Even in 1974, the decision to give Kurt Ritalin was contentious, with some scientists claiming it causes a Pavlovian response in children and increases the likelihood of addictive behaviour later in life; others believe that if children are not treated for hyperactivity, they may later self-medicate with illegal drugs. Kurt's diagnosis and whether the short period of medication benefited or injured him were different for each member of the Cobain family, but Kurt's own opinion, as he subsequently informed Courtney Love, was that the drug was significant. Love, who was taken Ritalin as a child, said the two talked about it a lot. "If you're a kid and you get this drug that makes you feel that way, where are you going to turn as an adult?""Love inquired. "Wasn't it euphoric when you were a kid? Isn't that memory going to stay with you?""

Wendy filed for divorce from Don in February 1976, only a week after Kurt's ninth birthday. She declared this one weeknight and rushed off in her Camaro, leaving Don to explain to the kids, which he didn't do well. Though Don and Wendy's marital problems had worsened in the latter half of 1974, her statement caught Don and the rest of the family off guard. Don withdrew into denial and moved inward, a habit that his son would emulate in times of difficulty years later. Don was surprised Wendy intended to tear up the family unit, despite her strong personality and occasional episodes of fury. Her primary issue was that he was constantly interested in sports—he was a referee, a coach, and a member of several teams. "In my mind, I didn't believe it was going to happen," Don said. "Divorce was not as common back then. I, too, did not want it to happen. She simply desired to leave."

Don moved out and took a room in Hoquiam on March 1. He rented by the week since he expected Wendy's rage to dissipate and their marriage to endure. Don saw his family as a significant part of his identity, and his role as a father marked one of the first times in his life when he felt needed. "He was crushed by the idea of divorce," Stan Targus, Don's best friend, recalled. Wendy's family admired Don, notably her sister Janis and her husband Clark, who lived close to the Cobains. Wendy's siblings questioned discreetly how she would manage financially without Don.

On March 29, Don was served with a summons and a "Petition for Dissolution of Marriage." A flood of court filings would follow, and Don would regularly neglect to react, hoping Wendy would change her mind. He was declared in default on July 9 for failing to respond to Wendy's requests. On the same day, a final settlement was granted, awarding Wendy the house but putting Don on the hook for $6,500 if the house was sold, Wendy remarried, or Kim turned eighteen. Don was given his 1965 Ford half-ton pickup truck, and Wendy was given the family's 1968 Camaro.

Wendy was granted custody of the children, but Don was ordered to pay $150 a month in child support, plus their medical and dental bills, and was granted "reasonable visitation" rights. The mechanics of visiting were not laid out in this small-town court in the 1970s, and the arrangement was informal. Don moved into his folks' Montesano trailer. Even after the formal paperwork was completed, he hoped Wendy would change her mind.

Wendy was having none of it. She was over something when she was finished with it, and she couldn't have been more over Don. She instantly fell for Frank Franich, a gorgeous longshoreman who earned twice as much as Don. Franich was also prone to violence and rage, and Wendy relished seeing that hatred directed at Don. When Don's new driver's licence was unintentionally shipped to Wendy's residence, someone opened it, wiped poop on Don's photo, resealed it, and forwarded it to Don. This wasn't a divorce; it was a blood feud filled with hatred, disdain, and vengeance.

It was an emotional catastrophe for Kurt—no other single incident in his life had a greater impact on the development of his personality. As many youngsters do, he internalised the divorce. The complexity of his parents' disputes had mostly been kept from him, and he couldn't comprehend why they had divorced. "He thought it was his fault, and he shouldered much of the blame," she said. "It was traumatic for Kurt, as he saw everything he trusted in—his security, family, and his own maintenance—unravel in front of his eyes." Kurt went inward rather than show his agony and sadness externally. Kurt scrawled on his bedroom wall in June, "I hate Mom, I hate Dad." Dad despises Mom, and Mom despises Dad. This was a youngster who, as a newborn, was so attached to his family that he battled sleep, as Mari had written in her home economics report seven years before, because "he doesn't want to leave them." Now, through no fault of his own, he had been abandoned. Kurt Cobain once said that 1976 was "Kurt's year in purgatory."

Kurt was also physically exhausted. Mari remembered Kurt being in the hospital at the time; she'd heard from her mother that he was there due to not eating enough. "I remember Kurt being in the hospital because of malnutrition when he was ten," she told me. Kurt informed his buddies that he needed to consume barium and get his stomach X-rayed. It's probable that what was initially misdiagnosed as starvation was actually the first sign of a stomach condition that would trouble him later in life. Kurt's mother had suffered from irritable bowel syndrome in her early twenties, not long after his birth, and when he initially started suffering stomachaches, it was presumed he had the same ailment as Wendy. Kurt had an involuntary twitching in his eyes around the time of the divorce. The family assumed it was due to stress, which it most likely was.

While his parents were separating, his life as a pre-adolescent kid continued, with all of its inherent struggles. As he approached fourth grade, he began to view girls as sexual creatures and became

23

concerned about his social standing. He was featured in the Aberdeen Daily World in July when his baseball club earned first place in the Aberdeen Timber League with a record of fourteen wins and one loss. His adoption of a black kitten that had been wandering about the neighbourhood was another highlight of the summer. Puff was his first pet, and he named it after himself.

Kurt indicated an interest in living with his father three months after the divorce was finalised. He moved in with Don, Leland, and Iris in the trailer, but by early fall, father and son had rented their own single-wide trailer across the street. Kurt spent his weekends with Wendy, Kim, and Puff.

Kurt's emotional needs were met by living with his father—he was once again the centre of attention as an only child. Don was so upset by the divorce that he overcompensated with expensive presents, purchasing Kurt a Yamaha Enduro-80 mini-bike, which quickly became a neighbourhood magnet. Kurt first met Lisa Rock, who lived a few blocks away, that fall: "He was a quiet, very likeable kid." Always with a friendly smile. He was a little reserved. There was this area where he'd ride his mini-bike, and I'd ride my bicycle alongside him."

Rock's description of the nine-year-old Kurt as "quiet" resembled a phrase that would be used to characterise him often in adulthood. He could sit in silence for long periods of time without feeling the need to make small talk. Kurt and Lisa shared a tenth birthday, and they celebrated by throwing a party at her place. Kurt was pleased to be invited, yet he was hesitant and uneasy with the attention. As a four-year-old, he was fearless; as a ten-year-old, he was surprisingly scared. He was reserved after the divorce, constantly waiting for the other person to make the first move.

Kurt's father assumed a more prominent role following the divorce and the onset of adolescence. Kurt would stay at his grandparents' house after school, but as soon as Don got home from work, they were together the rest of the day, and Kurt was glad to do anything Don wanted, even if it meant sports. After baseball games, the two Cobain brothers would eat dinner together at a neighbourhood malt store. It was a bonding experience that they both enjoyed, but they couldn't help but feel the loss of family-it was as if a limb had been cut, and while they got through the day without it, it was never far from their thoughts. Their love for each other was stronger than ever that year, yet both father and son were still deeply lonely. Kurt, fearful of losing his father, implored Don to vow not to remarry. Don assured his son that the two of them will always be together.

Kurt transferred to Beacon Elementary School in Montesano during the winter of 1976. Montesano's schools were smaller than Aberdeen's, and within weeks of transferring, he found a popularity that had previously eluded him, as well as a return of his fearlessness. Despite his outward confidence, he was bitter about his situation: "You could tell he was tormented by his parents' divorce," classmate Darrin Neathery observed.

Kurt was a fixture in "Monte," as locals called the town, by the time he started fifth grade in the fall of 1977-every student in the small school knew him, and most liked him. "He was a good-looking kid," John Fields said. "He was smart, and he had everything going for him." Kurt, with his blond hair and blue eyes, became a girl's favourite. "It was no exaggeration to say that he was one of the most popular kids," Roni Toyra remarked. "There was a group of about fifteen kids who would hang out together, and he was a big part of that." With his blond hair, beautiful blue eyes, and freckles on his nose, he was incredibly cute."

That outward appeal concealed a struggle for identity, which reached a new high in October 1977, when Don began dating. Kurt didn't care for the first lady Don met, so his father dumped her. Kurt didn't understand his father's yearning for adult company or why Don wasn't content with just the two of them because of his ten-year-old's narcissism. Don met Jenny Westby in late fall, who was divorced with two children: Mindy, a year younger than Kurt, and James, five years younger. Their romance was always a family affair, and their first date was a trek around Lake Sylvia with all of their children. Kurt was nice to Jenny and her kids, and Don thought he'd found his match. He and Jenny tied the knot.

Kurt liked Jenny at first because she gave him the female attention he craved, but his favourable sentiments for his new stepmother were tempered by an internal conflict: if he cared for her, he would be betraying his love for his mother and his "real" family. Kurt, like his father, had hoped that the divorce was only a momentary setback, a dream that would pass. His father's remarriage, as well as the now-extremely cramped trailer, shattered that illusion. Don wasn't a man of many words, and his upbringing made it tough for him to explain himself. "You told me you weren't going to get married again," Kurt remarked to Don. "Well, Kurt, you know, things change," his father said.

Jenny attempted to contact him but was unsuccessful. "At the beginning, he had a lot of affection toward everybody," she said. Later, Kurt continued withdrawing and referring to Don's commitment not to remarry. Don and Jenny tried to compensate by making Kurt the centre of attention around the house—he got to receive presents first and was given more leniency on chores—but these minor concessions only served to exacerbate his emotional detachment. He enjoyed playing with his step-siblings on occasion, but he also ridiculed them and was nasty to Mindy over her overbite, viciously imitating her voice in front of her.

Things improved temporarily when the family moved into their own home at 413 Fleet Street South in Montesano. Kurt had his own room, which was designed with round windows to resemble a ship. Jenny gave birth to another son, Chad Cobain, not long after the transfer. Two other children, a stepmother, and a baby were now fighting for Kurt's undivided attention.

Kurt had unrestricted access to Monte's parks, alleyways, and fields. It was a little town with no need for transportation; the baseball field was four blocks away, school was only up the road, and all of his pals were within walking distance. In comparison to Aberdeen, Monte reminded me of a Thornton Wilder play, a simpler and gentler America. Every Wednesday was family night at the Cobain home. Board games like Parcheesi and Monopoly were among the activities, and Kurt was just as enthused about them as everyone else.

Most vacations were camping excursions because money was scarce, but Kurt was the first person in the car when they were getting ready. His sister Kim accompanied them on their trips until Don and Wendy fought over whether vacations meant less child support; after that, Kim saw less of her father and brother. Kurt continued to visit his mother on weekends, but instead of pleasant reunions, these visits tended to aggravate the old wound of the divorce; Wendy and Don were scarcely polite, so trips to Aberdeen meant having to watch his two parents fight over the visitation schedule. Another tragedy befell him one weekend when Puff, his beloved cat, ran away and was never found.

Kurt, like other youngsters, was a creature of habit, and he relished the structure of activities such as family night. Even this modest consolation left him conflicted: he craved connection while afraid that getting close would lead to abandonment down the future. He'd reached adolescence, when most adolescent guys start to distinguish themselves from their parents, searching for their own identity. Kurt, on the other hand, was still grieving the loss of the original family nest, so breaking away was loaded with both necessity and fear. He dealt with his many contradictory emotions by emotionally distancing himself from Don and Wendy. He told himself and his pals that he despised them, and by doing so, he was able to rationalise his own estrangement. But after an afternoon of hanging out with his friends and complaining about his nasty parents, he'd find himself partaking in family night yet again, and being the only one in the home who didn't want the evening's festivities to finish.

Holidays were always an issue. Kurt was shuttled around to a half dozen different houses for Thanksgiving and Christmas in 1978. His sentiments for Jenny were a mix of fondness, envy, and betrayal, whereas his feelings for Wendy's boyfriend, Frank Franich, were pure rage. Wendy began to drink heavily as well, and the alcohol made her more caustic. Wendy was hospitalised after Franich fractured her arm one night—Kim was at the house and witnessed the incident. She refused to seek charges after she recovered. Wendy's brother Chuck threatened Franich, but there was little anyone could do to change her mind about him. Many people assumed Wendy stayed with Franich because of the financial support he gave. She'd started working as a clerk at Pearson's, an Aberdeen department store, after the divorce, but it was Franich's longshoreman salary that allowed them to afford luxuries like cable television. Wendy had been so far behind on her bills that her power was ready to be switched off before Franich arrived.

Kurt was eleven at the time, little and thin, but he had never felt more powerless or weak as when he was around Franich. He was powerless to protect his mother, and the stress of witnessing these confrontations made him fear for her and maybe for his own life. He pitied his mother and despised her for making him pity her. His parents had once been his gods; now they were fallen idols, false gods, and not to be trusted.

Kurt's behaviour began to reflect these internal conflicts. He argued with parents, refused to complete chores, and, despite his little stature, proceeded to abuse another youngster so severely that the victim refused to attend class. Teachers and parents became involved, and everyone questioned what had happened to such a sweet youngster. Don and Jenny finally took Kurt to counselling when they were at their wits' end. There was an attempt at family therapy, but Don and Wendy could never make it to the same appointment at the same time. The therapist, on the other hand, spent several sessions chatting with Kurt. Kurt, he concluded, needed a single family. "We were told if he was going to be with us, we needed to get legal custody of him, so that he knew we were accepting of him as part of our family," she said. "Unfortunately, all this did was to cause problems between Don and Wendy, as they debated it."

Don and Wendy had been divorced for several years, yet their animosity for each other persisted and even worsened via their children. Wendy had had a tough spring—her father, Charles Fradenburg, had died suddenly of a heart attack ten days after his 61st birthday. Wendy's mother, Peggy, had always been a loner, and Wendy was concerned that this would further isolate her mother. Peggy's unusual behaviour could be the outcome of a gruesome childhood occurrence in which her father stabbed himself in the abdomen in front of his family when she was ten years old. James Irving survived the suicide attempt and was sent to the same Washington psychiatric hospital where actress Frances Farmer later received shock therapy. He died two months later from his original injuries; while no one was looking, he ripped apart his stab wounds. Kurt's great-grandfather's mental condition, like many of the family's misfortunes, was discussed only in whispers.

Even the Fradenburg family's trials could not bring Don and Wendy together in shared anguish. Their discussions regarding Kurt ended with a fight, as did all of their interactions. Wendy eventually signed a contract that stated, "Donald Leland Cobain shall be solely responsible for the care, support, and maintenance of said child." Don was granted legal custody of Kurt on June 18, 1979, three weeks shy of three years following Don and Wendy's divorce.

3:

Meatball of the Month

Kurt started seventh grade at Montesano Junior High School in September 1979. It was a significant turning point in his life, and school began to play a larger role in his life. He had started music lessons in fifth grade and was playing drums in the school band by seventh grade, an accomplishment he tried to minimise to his buddies while simultaneously appreciating. The majority of what he studied and rehearsed was marching band or small ensemble drums, studying snare and bass drum for songs like "Louie, Louie" and "Tequila." The Monte band rarely marched, instead preferring to play for assemblies or basketball games, but Kurt was a mainstay at any event where they appeared.

Tim Nelson, his band director, described him as "a regular, run-of-the-mill music student." Kurt was pictured playing snare drum at an assembly in the Montesano "Sylvan" yearbook that year. He wore a pageboy hairstyle and resembled a young Brad Pitt. His wardrobe was preppy, consisting of Hash bell bottom jeans, a striped Izod rugby shirt, and Nike sports sneakers. He dressed like any other twelve-year-old, despite being a little short and undersized for his age.

He was chosen to be profiled in the October 26, 1979, edition of the mimeographed student newspaper, the Puppy Press, as one of the more popular kids at school. The item was titled "Meatball of the Month" and stated:

Kurt attends our school and is in seventh grade. He has blue eyes and blonde hair. He thinks school is fine. Band is Kurt's favourite class, and Mr. Hepp is his favourite teacher. Pizza and Coke are his favourite foods and beverages. His favourite phrase is "excuse me," his favourite song is "Don't Bring Me Down," and his favourite rock band is Meatloaf. Burt Reynolds is his favourite actor and "Taxi" is his favourite TV show.

Kurt's spin on Steve Martin's "excuse me" was typical with his sardonic, sarcastic sense of humour, which included transposing phrases or asking odd rhetorical questions—imagine an adolescent Andy Rooney. One of his favourite jokes was when he said over a bonfire, "How can you ruin a perfectly good fire by making smoke?""As a small boy, his way of surviving in the adolescent male culture was to joke his way out of conflicts and belittle any tormentors with his superior intellect."

Kurt sat in front of the television for several hours. Don and Jenny were fighting a losing battle; they wanted to limit his time in front of the tube, but he begged and shouted for more. When he was denied this freedom, he'd simply go to his best friend Rod Marsh's house, which was only a block away, and watch television there. Despite the fact that "Saturday Night Live" was past his bedtime, he seldom missed a week, and the following Monday at school he'd be copying all the best sketches. He also did an excellent rendition of Andy Kaufman's character Latka from "Taxi."

Kurt had dropped out of Little League the previous summer, but when winter arrived, he joined the junior varsity wrestling team, much to his father's delight. Don was at every game and constantly questioned Kurt about his progress. Kinichi Kanno, a Monte art teacher, was the coach, and Kurt joined the team to spend more time with Kanno than to wrestle. Kurt discovered a male role model in Kanno who encouraged his inventiveness, and he quickly became Kanno's favourite student. Kurt's drawing was featured on the front of the Puppy Press that Halloween, depicting Montesano's mascot, a bulldog, dumping a trick-or-treat bag on a doghouse. In true Cobain fashion, he hid a can of beer amid the chocolates. Kurt produced a pen-and-ink image of a tiny boy attempting to fish but casting the hook into his back for a Christmas card that year; it was as nice as most Hallmark cards. Kurt's artwork was "always very good," according to classmate Nikki Clark. Kanno never had to assist him since he appeared to be an accomplished student." Even when Kurt wasn't in art class, Clark recalled, he was never far from a pen: "He doodled incessantly in every class."

His doodles were largely of vehicles, trucks, and guitars, but he soon started making his own crude pornography. "He once showed me this sketch that he'd drawn," classmate Bill Burghardt recalled, "and it was a totally realistic picture of a vagina." 'What's it,' I questioned.Kurt had never seen a vagina up close before, except in literature or the sexual magazines the boys swapped. His second specialty was Satan, whom he drew in his notepad during every session.

Kurt's seventh-grade sweetheart was Roni Toyra, although it was a harmless first crush that never developed into anything serious. He presented her with a work of his art to symbolise their union. "There were kids in school that clearly were troubled or were outcasts, but he wasn't one of them," she told me. "The only thing that set him apart was that he was quieter than most kids." He wasn't unsociable; he was simply silent."

At home, he was anything but silent, ranting about what he saw as unfair treatment from Don or Jenny. Few second marriages with children ever work out perfectly, but this one was always on shaky ground, with questions of partiality and justice haunting the family. Kurt's criticisms generally sparked conflicts between Don and Jenny or heightened his parents' animosity, which lingered over issues of visitation and child support. Don stated that Wendy called him whenever his support check was a day late.

Kurt's proportions were borderline for scoliosis, or spinal curvature, according to the school nurse around the end of seventh grade. Kurt was taken to the doctor by Don and Jenny, and after a thorough examination, the doctor decided that Kurt did not have the syndrome—he simply had longer arms than other kids his size, which made the previous measurements appear off. This, however, did not reassure Wendy. She had learned Kurt had scoliosis through the family communication system, which resembled a terrible version of the children's game of telephone. She was surprised that Don wasn't concerned and that Kurt wasn't wearing a full-body cast. Kurt chose to believe his mother's diagnosis and later claimed he had "minor scoliosis in junior high." Despite the fact that his claim contradicts the facts, Kurt used it as yet more example of how his father had failed him.

Kurt, like many divorced children, expertly played each parent off the other. Wendy was working at the County Commissioner's Office in Monte in 1980, and Kurt frequently visited her after school, if only to report on some fresh cruelty inflicted on him by Don or Jenny. Kurt hoped Wendy would take him back as things deteriorated in Monte. But his mother was having troubles with Frank Franich at the time. She informed Kim that she was afraid Kurt might become gay if he saw the dysfunction in her home. Kurt's mother informed him years later, when he brought up the subject with Wendy and Kim, "Kurt, you don't even know what it was like." You would have been sent to juvie or jail."

Kurt frequently complained to Wendy about Jenny's children being given preferential treatment in the household. Kurt was envious when Jenny's ex-husband gave Mindy and James gifts. Kurt felt whatever punishment he received was because he wasn't Jenny's biological child. He told his pals he despised Jenny, grumbled about her cuisine, and said she rationed the amount of soda he could drink. He claimed Jenny could "hear a Pepsi can open from three rooms away," and he was only permitted "two slices of Carl Buddig ham per sandwich, and two Grandma's Cookies" for lunch.

"There could be fruit on the table, and Mindy or James could go up

34

and take an apple and start eating it," Leland Cobain would lecture Don about what he thought was a prejudice toward Kurt. Kurt would go get one like that, and Donnie would give him grief for it." Leland felt that Don sided with Jenny and her children because he was scared Jenny would leave him, like Wendy had. Don recognized that Kurt had a more difficult time with discipline than Jenny's children, but contended that this was due to Kurt's personality, not favouritism. Don, on the other hand, was concerned that Jenny would leave him if Kurt caused too much trouble: "I was afraid that it was going to get to the point of 'either he goes or she goes,' and I didn't want to lose her."

As he grew older, Kurt's relationship with his brothers and step-siblings became more balanced. Because he loves babies, he cherished his half-brother Chad. He'd punch Mindy, but when school wasn't in session, he'd spend the day playing with her. When Kurt's classmates mentioned his family-and several of them thought Mindy was cute-he was quick to correct them if they called her his "sister." He described Mindy to his classmates as "not my sister-my dad's new wife's daughter," speaking the words as if she were some torture he had to endure.

Kurt and James got along better, possibly because Kurt was never overshadowed by the younger brother. When another child slugged James, the bat-boy on one of Kurt's baseball teams, he intervened and threatened the assailant. They also had a common passion in movies. The family would travel to a two-screen drive-in throughout the summer. Don and Jenny would each take a car, then park one with the kids in front of a PG-rated movie and the other with an adult picture. Instead of sitting through another Don Knotts comedy, Kurt taught James that they could stroll to the lavatory and see more adult fare—like Heavy Metal, which Kurt loved-by standing just outside the lot. Kurt enjoyed telling his younger stepbrother about movies he had already seen. He'd seen Close Encounters of the Third Kind the year before and knew every line of dialogue. "He used to play with his mashed potatoes at dinner and make them into the shape of the mountain from that movie," he said.

Kurt began making his own short films in 1981, when he was fourteen, using his parents' Super-8 camera. One of his early films was an elaborate rip-off of Orson Welles' War of the Worlds, in which aliens landed in Kurt Cobain's backyard, performed by characters Kurt fashioned with clay. He successfully persuaded James that their home had been attacked by aliens by showing him the alien DVD. Another film he created in 1982, Kurt Commits Bloody Suicide, exposes a considerably darker aspect of his psyche: in it, Kurt, playing to a camera held by James, pretends to cut his wrists with the edge of a torn-in-half pop can. The film includes special effects, artificial blood, and Kurt acting out his own last dying scene in the manner he must have seen in silent films.

This violent film merely reinforced his parents' anxieties about the darkness they perceived within him. "There was something wrong," Jenny contended, "something wrong with his thought process from the beginning, something unbalanced." He was able to narrate situations that would give most young boys nightmares: murder, rape, suicide. He wasn't the first adolescent to make light of suicide, but the casual way he did so struck his peers as unusual. When he and John Fields were walking home from school one day, Fields suggested Kurt become an artist, but Kurt nonchalantly declared, "I'm going to be a superstar musician, kill myself, and go out in a flame of glory," he claimed. "Kurt, that's the stupidest thing I ever heard-don't talk that way," Fields said. Kurt, on the other hand, was adamant: "No, I want to be rich and famous and kill myself like Jimi Hendrix." Neither boy realized at the time that Hendrix's death was not a suicide. Fields was not Kurt's only Monte buddy who told such a story; a half dozen other acquaintances relate identical versions of the same conversation, all with the same tragic result.

Nobody in the family was surprised when Kurt casually mentioned suicide at the age of fourteen. Two years earlier, Kurt's great-uncle, 66-year-old Burle Cobain, Leland's oldest brother, had shot himself in the stomach and head with a snub-nose.38 revolver. Leland had found the body. There were reports that Burle was set to face sexual molestation charges. Burle wasn't as connected to the family as Kurt's other uncles, but he was often talking about it with his friends. He would casually remark that his uncle had "killed himself over the death of Jim Morrison," despite the fact that Morrison had died a decade ago.

What had seemed like a joke to Kurt turned out to be a crushing blow to Leland. Leland's brother Ernest died of a brain hemorrhage a year before Burle's suicide, in 1978. While Ernest's death at the age of 57 was not officially considered a suicide, it occurred after he had been warned that if he continued to drink, he would die. He persisted, and eventually tumbled down the stairs, producing the fatal aneurysm.

Kurt was affected by more than just these tragedies. A Montesano boy hanged himself outside one of the primary schools when Kurt was in eighth grade. Kurt recognized him; he was Bill Burghardt's younger brother. Kurt, Burghardt, and Rod Marsh saw the body hanging from a tree on their way to school and stared at it for half an hour before school administrators shooed them away. "It was the most grotesque thing I ever saw in my life," Marsh recalled. Suicide became an idea and a phrase that was no longer taboo, thanks to Kurt's family history and this tragedy. It was simply a part of his environment, like drunkenness, poverty, or narcotics. Kurt revealed to Marsh that he has "suicide genes."

Kurt began experimenting with drugs in the eighth grade, when he began smoking marijuana and used LSD. He began smoking marijuana at parties, then with his buddies, and then on a regular basis by himself. He was a full-fledged pothead by ninth grade. Marijuana was cheap and plentiful in Monte, with the majority of it being homegrown, and it helped Kurt forget about his home life. What began as a social ritual evolved into his preferred anaesthetic.

When he first started using narcotics, he also began skipping class on a regular basis. When he and his companions skipped school, they would buy pot or take alcohol from someone's parents' liquor cabinet. Kurt, on the other hand, began skipping school on his own or attending but leaving after the first period. He saw less of his pals and appeared to be disconnected from everything save his own rage. On New Year's Eve 1980, Trevor Briggs found Kurt alone at a park in Monte, swinging on a swing and humming. Trevor brought Kurt to his parents' place, where the two smoked marijuana while watching Dick Clark on TV. The year finished with both of them puking after smoking too much home-grown marijuana.

What had appeared like a lovely location to go to school just a few years before has quickly become Kurt's own brand of prison. He now trashed Monte and his parents in chats with his pals. He had recently finished Harper Lee's "To Kill a Mockingbird," and he thought it was a wonderful representation of the town. By the beginning of 1981, a new Kurt was beginning to emerge, or not emerge, as was more often the case: he was spending greater amounts of time alone. He had relocated to a refurbished basement bedroom in the Fleet Street home. Kurt told his buddies that the shift felt like a punishment. Kurt spent his time in his basement room with a Montgomery Ward's pinball machine he'd gotten for Christmas, a stereo Don and Jenny had passed down to him, and a stack of albums. Elton John, Grand Funk Railroad, and Boston were among the artists represented in the record collection. Journey's Evolution was Kurt's favourite album that year.

His disagreements with Don and Jenny had reached a boiling point. All of their attempts to entice him to join the family were futile. He had begun to boycott family night and, feeling abandoned internally, had resolved to abandon his family outwardly. "We had chores for him, just typical stuff, but he wouldn't do them," Don recalled. "He didn't." "We started bribing him with an allowance, but if he didn't do certain chores, we'd deduct from it." But he refused to take any action. As a result, he owes us money. He'd become agitated, bang doors, and storm downstairs." He also appeared to have fewer pals. "I noticed that some of his friends were dropping off," Jenny told me. "He was home a lot more, but even when he was home, he wasn't with us." He appeared to become much more introverted. Kurt was quiet and moody," Rod Marsh recalled, recalling Kurt murdering a neighbour's cat that year. In this instance of adolescent sadism that would contrast sharply with his adult life, he trapped the still-alive animal in his parents' chimney and laughed when it died and stunk up the home.

Kurt started his first year of high school in Montesano in September 1981. In an attempt to blend in, he joined the football squad that fall. Despite his small stature, he made the initial cut-an indication, more than anything else, of how small Montesano was. He practised for two weeks before dropping out, claiming it was too much work. He also joined the track team that year. He was able to throw the discus and run the 200-yard dash despite his small stature. He wasn't the finest athlete on the team-he missed a lot of practices-but he was one of the quicker kids. He was depicted straining into the sun in the squad's yearbook shot.

In February of that year, Uncle Chuck surprised Kurt by telling him he could have either a bicycle or an electric guitar for his fourteenth birthday. It was no choice for a child who drew images of rock stars in his notebook. Kurt had previously ruined Don's Hawaiian lap guitar, taking it apart to analyse its internal workings. Chuck's guitar wasn't much better: it was a cheap, second-hand Japanese model. It frequently shattered, but to Kurt, it was the air he breathed. He contacted Aunt Mari and inquired if it was strung alphabetically because he didn't know how to put the strings on it. When he got it operating, he played it all the time and took it to school to show off. "Everyone asked him about it," Trevor Briggs recalled. "I saw him with it on the street, and he told me, 'Don't ask me to play any songs on this; it's broken.'" That didn't matter-it wasn't so much an instrument as it was a way of life.

Athletics were also a component of his identity; he had persisted with wrestling as a freshman, eventually making the varsity squad. The Montesano Bulldogs won the league championship that year, with a record of twelve victories and three losses, despite Kurt's absence. He'd started skipping more practices and games, and his size was a big disadvantage on the varsity team. Wrestling was a fun way to roughhouse on the JV team two years before; the varsity team, on the other hand, was deadly serious, and practices required him to wrestle males who promptly pinned him. Kurt sat for the team portrait at the end of the season wearing knee-high striped socks— among the team's behemoths, he looked more like the trainer than a member of the squad.

Kurt had one of his most memorable confrontations with his father on the varsity wrestling mat. According to Kurt, he went out onto the ring on the day of a title match to deliver a message to Don in the bleachers. Kurt later told Michael Azerrad, "I waited for the whistle to blow, just staring straight into [Don's] face, and then I instantly clammed up-I put my arms together, and let the guy pin me." Kurt claimed he did this four times in a row, and each time, he was pinned instantly, and Don walked out in disgust. Don Cobain claimed the story was bogus; Kurt's classmates claim they don't remember it and say that anyone who lost on purpose would have been shunned, if not battered, by their teammates. But, after the match, Leland Cobain remembered Don telling him the story, remarking, "That little shit just laid there." He was not going to fight back."

Kurt was an expert at inflating a story in order to convey an emotional truth rather than an actual one. What most likely happened was that Kurt had a match against a stronger opponent and chose not to fight back, which enraged his fastidious father. However, Kurt's retelling of the story, as well as his depiction of the look that flashed between him and his father, show how far their relationship had deteriorated in the six years following the divorce. They used to spend every spare hour together, and Kurt had never loved someone more on the day Don bought the mini-bike. Just down the road from Montesano High School was a restaurant where they used to sit-the two of them alone, a singular entity, a family-and eat a quiet dinner together, joined in their loneliness; a little boy who wanted nothing more than to spend the rest of his life with his father, and a father who only wanted someone to love him with an unfading love. Six years later, however, father and son were embroiled in a battle of wills, and, as with all great tragedies, neither combatant thought he could afford to lose. Kurt needed a father figure, and Don wanted to be wanted by his son, but neither could confess it.

It was a tragedy of Shakespearean proportions; no matter how far Kurt moved away from the wrestling mat, in the corner of his eye, he was always looking directly at his father, or, to be more accurate, looking at his father's ghost, since his relationship with his father was virtually dead to him after this point. Kurt would fire off a harsh lyric in a song named "Serve the Servants," the words yet another move in his never-ending battle with his biggest opponent: "I tried hard to have a father, but instead I had a dad."

4:

Prairie Belt Sausage Boy

Kurt left 413 Fleet Street and his father and stepmother's care in March 1982 at his own request. Kurt would spend the next few years bouncing around Grays Harbor's figurative wilderness. Though he'd make two year-long breaks, he'd spend the following four years living in ten different houses with ten different families. None of them would be comfortable.

His first stop was outside Montesano, at his paternal grandparents' trailer. He could take the bus into Monte every morning, allowing him to stay in the same school and class, but even his peers recognized that the shift was difficult. He had the sympathetic ear of his beloved Iris at his grandparents', and there were times when he and Leland shared closeness, but he spent much of his time alone. It was only one more step toward a larger, more profound loneliness.

He once assisted his grandfather in building a dollhouse for Iris's birthday. Kurt helped by painstakingly stapling miniature cedar shingles to the structure's roof. Kurt made a rough chess set out of leftover wood. He started by drawing the shapes of the pieces on the wood, then whittling them with a knife. Kurt's grandfather demonstrated how to use the jigsaw halfway through the process, then left the fifteen-year-old to his own devices while observing from the door. When the youngster looked up at his grandfather for affirmation, Leland would say, "Kurt, you're doing good."

But Leland's words were not always kind, and Kurt found himself in the same father/son situation he'd experienced with Don. Leland was ready to criticise his decrees to Kurt. Kurt, in Leland's defence, could be a real nuisance. With so many different parental figures—and none with ultimate power over him—he finally wore out his elders when his adolescent years began. His family portrayed a picture of a defiant and obstinate youngster who refused to listen to elders or work. In contrast to everyone else in his family—even his younger sister Kim had helped pay the bills with her paper route—petulance and idleness appeared to be an essential element of his temperament. "Kurt was lazy," his uncle Jim Cobain recounted. "Whether it was simply because he was a typical teenager or because he was depressed, no one knew."

Kurt departed Montesano in the summer of 1982 to live with Uncle Jim in South Aberdeen. His uncle was taken aback when he was handed the task. "I was shocked that they would let him live with me," Jim Cobain recalled. "I was smoking marijuana at the time." I was completely unaware of his requirements, let alone what the hell I was doing." Despite his inexperience, Jim was not a harsh disciplinarian. "I had a really nice stereo system and lots of records by the Grateful Dead, Led Zeppelin, and the Beatles," he said, two years younger than his brother Don. And I'd crank that baby up loud." Rebuilding an amplifier was Kurt's greatest thrill during his months with Jim.

Jim and his wife had an infant girl and requested Kurt to leave soon after. Kurt then moved in with Wendy's siblings and sisters. "Kurt was handed down from relative to relative," Jim explained. He was the stereotypical latchkey child. He got along better with his relatives and aunts than he did with his parents, but he still had authority issues. His uncles and aunts were less rigorous, but there was less of an attempt at formal family connection in the more laid-back houses. His relatives had their own difficulties and struggles—there wasn't anyone who could give him space, both physically and emotionally, and Kurt knew it.

Kurt stayed with his Uncle Chuck for several months and began taking guitar lessons. Chuck was in a band with Warren Mason, one of the harbour's finest guitar players. When they practised at Chuck's house—rehearsals that always involved marijuana and a bottle of

Jack Daniel's—Kurt would stand in the corner, staring at Warren like a hungry guy looking at a meatball sandwich. Chuck asked Warren one day whether he might teach the boy, and thus Kurt's formal musical education began.

According to Kurt, he just took one or two lessons and learnt everything he needed to know in that short time. Warren, on the other hand, recalls the training going on for months and Kurt being a dedicated student who spent hours trying to apply himself. The first issue Warren had to deal with was Kurt's guitar, which was more for show than for performing. Warren discovered Kurt an Ibanez for $125. Lessons were $5 for half an hour. "What are some of the songs you want to learn?" Warren asked Kurt, as he did all of his young students." "Stairway to Heaven," Kurt said. Kurt already knew how to play a rough rendition of "Louie, Louie," and they worked on "Stairway" before moving on to AC/DC's "Back in Black." The lessons ended when Kurt's bad grades forced his uncle to reconsider their afternoon activity.

Kurt attended Monte High School until the second month of his sophomore year, when he switched to Weatherwax High School in Aberdeen. It was the same school his mother and father had attended, but despite his familial ties and proximity to his mother's house-it was only ten blocks away-he felt like an outsider there. Weatherwax, which opened in 1906, took up three city blocks and five unique buildings, and Kurt's class had 300 students-three times the size of Monte's. Kurt found himself in a school with four factions-stoners, jocks, preppies, and nerds-and he didn't fit into any of them at first. "Aberdeen was full of cliques," Rick Miller, another Monte transfer to Weatherwax, remarked. "Neither of us really knew anyone." Even though Aberdeen was Hicksville in comparison to Seattle, it was still a significant improvement from Monte. "We never knew where we fit in." Changing schools as a sophomore would have been stressful for most well-adjusted kids; it was agonising for Kurt.

While he'd been popular in Monte-a preppy in his Izod shirts, a jock due to his interest in sports-he was an outsider in Aberdeen. He maintained contact with his pals in Monte, but despite seeing them virtually every weekend, his sense of loneliness grew. He dropped out of sports since his athletic abilities were insufficient to give him prominence in a huge institution. His retreat from the world was exacerbated by his own self-doubt as a result of his damaged family and wandering existence. Later, Kurt would tell stories about being beaten up in Aberdeen and being subjected to incessant abuse at the hands of redneck high-school youths. His peers at Weatherwax, on the other hand, don't recall any such incidents—he magnified his emotional isolation into phantom tales of physical assault.

There was one saving grace in his studies: Weatherwax had a superb art department, and Kurt excelled in this one class. Bob Hunter, his teacher, thought he was an exceptional student because "he had both the ability to draw, coupled with a great imagination." Hunter let his students listen to the radio while they worked—he was an artist and musician himself—and encouraged them to be creative. He was the ideal instructor for Kurt, and like Mr. Kanno before him, he was one of the few adult role models the youngster could look up to.

Kurt took commercial art and basic art in the fifth and sixth periods his first year at Weatherwax. These two 50-minute lessons, scheduled shortly after lunch, were the only times he knew he'd be at school every day. Hunter was impressed and, at times, astounded by his ability. Kurt drew Michael Jackson with one gloved hand in the air and the other gripping his crotch for a caricature assignment. Kurt illustrated a sperm developing into an embryo during another lecture in which the students were required to describe an object as it evolved. His painting abilities were exceptional, but it was his twisted thinking that caught the attention of his peers. "That sperm was a shock to all of us," classmate Theresa Van Camp recalled. "It was a completely different mental attitude. People started talking about him, wondering, "What does he think of?"When Hunter advised Kurt that the Michael Jackson drawing would not be appropriate to exhibit in the school hallways, he sketched a nasty portrait of Ronald Reagan with a raisin-like face instead.

Kurt had always drawn feverishly, but with Hunter's support, he began to picture himself as an artist. His scribbles formed an important component of his schooling. He was skilled at cartooning, and it was through this that he first learned the art of storytelling. The exploits of "Jimmy, the Prairie Belt Sausage Boy," named after a canned sausage product, were a recurring cartoon from this time period. These stories chronicled Jimmy's (a thinly disguised Kurt) hard childhood growing up with strict parents. Kurt's difficulties with his father were depicted gently in one full-colour, multi-panel version. In the first panel, Jimmy is lectured by the father figure: "This oil is filthy." It smells like gas to me. You filthy little creep, get me a 9-mm wrench. If you're going to live here, you'll have to follow my standards, which are as serious as my moustache: honesty, loyalty, dedication, honour, heroism, severe discipline, God and nation, that's what makes America No. 1. One." Another cartoon depicts a mother yelling, "I'm having your son and aborting your daughter." PTA meeting at seven o'clock, pottery class at 2:30, steak stroganoff, dog to vet at three o'clock, laundry, yeah, yes, mmm honey, it feels wonderful in the ass, mmm, I love you."

It's unclear whether the mother in the animation is Jenny or Wendy, but attending Weatherwax also meant moving back in with his mother at 1210 East First Street. Kurt's upstairs room had remained unchanged, a tribute to past days within the nuclear family, and this was as close to a permanent home as he could get. He'd spent weekends here on and off, decorating the walls with band posters, many of which were now hand drawn. The nicest part of his room, and his life, was, of course, his guitar. Wendy's home was less crowded than his other trips during these years, allowing him to practise without interruption. However, the family situation was only slightly improved; his mother had finally broken loose from Frank Franich, but Kurt and Wendy were still arguing.

Wendy was a totally different mother from the one Kurt had left six years before. She was now 35 years old, yet she was dating younger guys and going through what could only be described as a mid-life crisis characteristic of recently divorced men. She was drinking a lot and had become a frequent at Aberdeen's many taverns, which was one of the reasons Kurt wasn't immediately returned to her care after Don left. That year, she began a casual relationship with Mike Medak, 22. Wendy didn't even mention having children with Medak during the first several months they saw each other; she usually stayed at his place, and he didn't see her children until several months into their relationship. "It was like she was a single woman," he recalled. "It wasn't like we were waiting for the babysitter on Friday night—it was as if there were no kids." Dating Wendy was like dating a 22-year-old. "We'd go to the local tavern or dancing club. And we'd party." Wendy grumbled about Franich breaking her arm, her financial difficulties, and Don's distance. One of the few stories she told about Kurt was how, at the age of five, he went into the living room with a hard-on in front of Don and his buddies. Don was humiliated and carried his son out of the room. Wendy chuckled as she recounted the episode, which had become family legend.

Medak was a 22-year-old dating a 35-year-old for physical reasons; Wendy was a lovely older woman, an ideal date if you weren't looking for commitment. Kurt, who was fifteen at the time, could sense it and was quick to judge. Kurt told his pals about his mother's dates, and his remarks were harsh, though they didn't address the psychological turmoil he must have felt witnessing his mother take a lover who was only seven years his senior. "He said he hated his mom, that he thought she was a slut," John Fields recalled. "He didn't agree with her way of life." He didn't like her at all, and he fantasised of fleeing. Kurt would leave the house if she was around because she yelled at him constantly."

Wendy's siblings recall being concerned about her drinking, but it was rarely discussed because their family communication style was non-confrontational.

Kurt found his mother's attractiveness to be an embarrassment. Wendy's propensity of sunbathing in a bikini in the garden had all of his buddies peering through the fence. When guests were over, they joked that if there wasn't enough room, they would gladly accept to sleep with Wendy. Kurt would punch anyone who made this joke, and he punches a lot. Wendy was particularly appealing to these young males because she would occasionally buy booze for them. "Kurt's mom bought us booze a couple of times," Mike Bartlett recalled. "It was with the understanding that we would drink it at the house." Wendy once paid for beer for the kids and allowed them to watch Pink Floyd's The Wall film. "We talked his mom into buying us a fifth of tequila one time when a few of us were spending the night there," Trevor Briggs said. We got intoxicated and went for a walk. Kurt's intoxicated, fifteen-year-old answer was to yell at his mom's paramour, "Give it up buddy! You're not going to get any. Return home!" It was a jest, but his longing for a more traditional household was far from amusing.

Kurt's top Christmas wish that year was the Oingo Boingo album Nothing to Fear. His aunt photographed him clutching it at the Fradenburg Christmas festivity. He appears considerably younger than fifteen, with his still-short hair and boyish features. Aunt Mari gave him the record Tadpoles by the Bonzo Dog Band, which included the novelty song "Hunting Tigers Out in Indiah," which Kurt loved that winter and learned to play on guitar. He'd gone to Mari, who'd moved to Seattle, just before Christmas to look for record stores. Kurt's wish list included a soundtrack album for the film "H. R. He enjoyed the television show "Pufnstuf." Another CD he sought was REO Speedwagon's Hi Infidelity, which his aunt had never heard of.

That February, he turned sixteen and passed his driver's test. But the most significant occurrence was that spring was far more significant to him than his learner's permit—it was a landmark he talked about continuously throughout youth, but never in maturity. Kurt attended his first concert, Sammy Hagar and Quarterflash, on March 29, 1983, at the Seattle Center Coliseum. Kurt and Darrin Neathery, whose elder sister drove them, were major fans of Seattle radio station KISW—the signal would come in clear at night—and he enjoyed Hagar's "butt rock" and Quarterflash's smash "Harden My Heart." "It was a big deal because it was the first concert we both saw," Neathery went on to say. "We got a six-pack of Schmidt somehow." Kurt and I sat in the backseat and had a great time on the trip up. When we arrived at the event, I recall standing on the floor in the back, where they did the lighting, after Quarterflash had finished. We were completely taken aback by the lighting and the production. Then a whiskey bottle shattered right past us from the very top stands. We almost peed our trousers. So we hauled out of there and sought a spot in the higher rafters to keep an eye on Sammy. Kurt and I both bought T-shirts." Kurt would later rewrite history and claim that his first gig was with the punk band Black Flag. However, every one of Kurt's Weatherwax classmates remembered the sixteen-year-old Kurt showing up to school the next day wearing an oversized Sammy Hagar T-shirt and speaking like a pilgrim who had just returned from the Holy Land.

Kurt found punk rock as the 1983 school year came to an end, and the Sammy Hagar T-shirt was relegated to the bottom drawer, never to be seen again. That summer, he saw the Melvins, and it was a life-changing experience. In his journal, he wrote:

In the summer of 1983, I was hanging out at a Montesano, Washington Thriftway when this short-haired employee box-boy, who resembled the man from Air Supply, handed me a brochure that read: "The Them Festival." Tomorrow night in the Thriftway parking lot. "Free live rock music." Monte was not used to having live rock performances in their small community of a few thousand loggers and their obedient wives. I arrived in a van with stoner companions. And there was the Air Supply box-boy, holding a Les Paul with a picture of Kool Cigarettes from a magazine on it. They played music quicker and with more enthusiasm than my Iron Maiden CDs could deliver. This was just what I needed. Punk rock, eh? The other stoners were bored and started yelling, "Play some Def Leppard." God, I hated those idiots more than ever. I arrived at the promised land of a grocery store parking lot and discovered my unique destiny.

He had twice emphasised "This was what I was looking for."

It was his aha moment—the moment when his narrow world suddenly expanded. Kurt had known the "Air Supply box-boy" as Roger "Buzz" Osborne, an aloof older kid at Montesano High. When Kurt congratulated Buzz after the show, he played on Osborne's vanity, and Buzz soon took on the role of mentor, sending along punk rock CDs, a book on the Sex Pistols, and dog-eared copies of Creem magazines. Despite his diary note, Kurt continued to attend Judas Priest concerts at the Tacoma Dome that summer. He blended his punk with a lot of heavy metal, like other kids in Aberdeen, though he didn't brag about it in front of Buzz, and he now preferred punk T-shirts.

The Melvins had started a year prior, mockingly calling themselves after another Thriftway employee. Buzz claims that he learned to play guitar by listening to the first two Clash albums. The Melvins had no true fan following in 1983; they were heckled and derided by the majority of Grays Harbor's metalheads. Nonetheless, a dozen impressionable teenagers would congregate around their rehearsal location, which was located behind drummer Dale Crover's house at 609 West Second in Aberdeen. This motley gang of fans was dubbed

"Cling-Ons," a term developed by Buzz to represent their "Star Trek"-like geekiness as well as their habit of clinging to every word he spoke. Buzz, with his white-man's afro, resembled Richard Simmons more than the fellow in Air Supply.

Buzz gave advice to the "Cling-Ons," recorded tapes for them, and served as the Socrates of Montesano, an elder statesman who lectured his band of followers on all things worldly. He selected who was permitted to practise and who was not, and he made up nicknames for everyone who was accepted. Jesse Reed, whom Kurt had met in class at Weatherwax and soon befriended, became "Black Reed" after the band Black Flag, despite the fact that he, like the rest of the crew, was Caucasian. Kurt never had a memorable moniker. His pals during this time period always called him "Cobain," and his absence of a nickname was not an indication that he was given special treatment. In reality, he didn't have a moniker because he was looked at as a runt who didn't deserve to be recognized.

The Melvins, like Kurt, stretched from Monte (where Buzz lived with his parents) to Aberdeen (Crover's practice area). Kurt had known the Melvins' bass player, Matt Lukin, from Monte, from wrestling and Little League, and he quickly became a friend. When Kurt went to Monte, he was more likely to look up Buzz or Lukin than his father.

One journey to Monte that summer was inspired by something other than his newfound passion for punk rock—it was motivated by a lady. Andrea Vance, Kurt's buddy Darrin Neathery's younger sister, was babysitting Monte one day when Kurt unexpectedly visited. "He was darling," she remembered. "He had amazing blue eyes and a killer smile." His hair was lovely and smooth. He had it cut to a medium length. He didn't say much, and when he did, it was in hushed tones." They watched "The Brady Bunch," and Kurt played Sock-and-Boots with the kids. He returned the next afternoon, as expected, and Vance rewarded him with a kiss. He came back every day for a week, but the romance never went beyond necking. "He was very sweet and really respectful," Vance recalls. "I didn't feel like he was a walking hormone."

But his hormones were roaring beneath the surface. That same summer, Kurt had his "first sexual encounter," with a developmentally handicapped girl. According to his notebook, he only sought her after getting so depressed about the status of his life that he considered suicide. "That month happened to be the epitome of my mental abuse from my mother," he stated in the letter. "It turned out that pot wasn't helping me escape my problems very well anymore, and I was actually enjoying doing rebellious things like stealing booze and busting store windows....I decided that within the next month, I'm not going to sit on my roof and fantasize about jumping, but I'm going to kill myself." And I wasn't leaving this earth without experiencing what it's like to be laid."

Trevor Briggs, John Fields, and Kurt followed her home one day and stole her father's vodka, which seemed to be his only option. They'd done it before, but this time Kurt lingered after his friends had left. He sat on her lap and stroked her breasts. She went into her bedroom and undressed in front of him, but he was disgusted with both himself and her. "I tried to fuck her, but I didn't know how," he said. "I got grossed out very heavily by how her vagina smelled and her sweat reeked, so I left." Though Kurt retreated, the embarrassment remained with him for the rest of his life. He hated himself for taking advantage of her, but he also despised himself for failing to see the situation through to intercourse, which was an even worse humiliation for a sixteen-year-old virgin. Kurt was named as a suspect when the girl's father complained to the school that his daughter had been assaulted. In his journal, he wrote, "They came with a yearbook and were going to have her pick me out, but she couldn't because I didn't show up for pictures that year." He claimed he was taken to the Montesano Police station and interrogated, but escaped conviction because the girl was over eighteen and "not mentally retarded" under legal statutes.

Kurt began his junior year at Weatherwax in Aberdeen by initiating a love relationship with fifteen-year-old Jackie Hagara. He planned it so they could walk to school together because she lived two streets away. He'd fallen so far behind in arithmetic that he'd been compelled to enrol in a freshman maths class, where they'd met. Despite the fact that many of the students in the class felt Kurt was odd for being put behind, Jackie appreciated his smile. He showed her a drawing he'd created of a rock star on a desolate island one day after school. The man was holding a Les Paul guitar that was connected into a palm tree with a Marshall stack. It was Kurt's idea of paradise at the age of sixteen.

Jackie expressed her appreciation for the drawing. He approached her two days later with a gift: he had redone the identical painting in billboard format, complete with airbrushing. "It's for you," he murmured, glancing down at the floor. "For me?" she inquired. "I'd like to go out with you sometime," he said. Kurt was just mildly disappointed when Jackie informed him that she already had a boyfriend. They continued to go to school together, holding hands on occasion, and one afternoon in front of her house, he pulled her close and kissed her. "I thought he was so cute," she commented.

During his key junior year, his appearance shifted from what had been unanimously recognized as "cute" to what some of his Weatherwax classmates would describe as "scary." He grew his hair long and rarely washed it. His Izod shirts and rugby pullovers had been replaced by homemade T-shirts with punk band names. One of the t-shirts he wore regularly said "Organised Confusion," a slogan he imagined would be the name of his first band. He always had a trench coat on hand for outerwear, and he wore it year round, whether it was raining or a hot summer day. Andrea Vance, Kurt's Monte girlfriend from that summer, ran into him at a party that fall and didn't remember him. "He had on his black trench coat, hi-top tennis shoes, and his hair was dyed dark red," she said. "He didn't look like the same boy."

His circle of friends gradually switched from Monte pals to Aberdeen pals, but both groups' major pastime was getting intoxicated in some fashion. When they couldn't raid their parents' booze supply, they'd ask one of Aberdeen's many street people to help them buy beer. Kurt, Jesse Reed, Greg Hokanson, and Eric and Steve Shillinger had a regular business relationship with "The Fat Man," a hopeless alcoholic who resided in the run-down Morck Hotel with his disabled son, Bobby. The Fat Man was willing to buy them beer in exchange for payment and assistance in getting to the store. This was a time-consuming operation that resembled a Buster Keaton play and might take all day: "First," Jesse Reed explained, "we had to push a shopping cart to the Morck." Then we'd go up to his room and help him get up. He'd be in his crusty underpants, which stank and was infested with flies, and it was dreadful. We'd have to assist him in putting on these tent trousers. We'd have to help him downstairs because he weighed roughly 500 pounds. We'd put him in the cart and push him since he was too big to walk all the way to the liquor store. We'd push him to the grocery store, which was mercifully closer, if we just wanted to drink beer. And all we had to do was buy a quart of the cheapest malt liquor for him."

The Fat Man and Bobby, a strange couple if ever there was one, unwittingly became the subjects of some of Kurt's stories. He created imagined songs about their experiences, wrote short novels about them, and drew them in his journal. Kurt's pencil drawing of the Fat Man resembled Ignatius J. Reilly, the anti-hero from John Kennedy Toole's "A Confederacy of Dunces." Kurt's friendship with the Fat Man and Bobby wasn't without affection; he felt sympathy for their seemingly hopeless condition. Kurt purchased the Fat Man, a toaster and a John Denver album from Goodwill for Christmas that year.

When the Fat Man grasped these gifts in his enormous mitt-hands, he said, "These are for me?"" He began to cry. The Fat Man spent the next few years in Aberdeen telling everyone what a great guy Kurt Cobain was. It was a modest indication of how, even in Kurt's shadow world, sweetness might be found.

Kurt continued to drink alcohol that spring, thanks to a steady supply of booze from the Fat Man, and his disputes with his mother grew as a result. When Kurt was stoned or fried on acid, which became a regular occurrence, the discussions were even more heated. Greg Hokanson recounted coming to Kurt's residence with Jesse Reed and hearing Wendy rage at Kurt for an hour while he was high on LSD and entirely unresponsive to her yells. "Wendy was awful to him," Hokanson admitted. "He hated her." As soon as they could, the trio left the house and headed to climb the water tower on "Think of Me Hill." Jesse and Hokanson reached it to the top, but Kurt froze halfway up the ladder. "He was too afraid," Hokanson recalls. Kurt was never able to scale the tower.

"I think she was a little intoxicated, and she came upstairs into his room," Trevor Briggs recalled one evening at the Cobains when Kurt and Wendy fought all night. She was attempting to party and have a good time with us. He was enraged at her for it. 'Kurt, if you don't watch it, I'm going to tell your buddies what you told me,' she continued, and he exclaimed loudly, 'What are you talking about?Eventually, she departed. So I inquired what she was going to say. 'Well, I made a statement to her once about how just because a person develops hair on his balls, doesn't imply he's a grown man or mature,' he explained." Having hair on your testicles was a huge source of humiliation for Kurt. His pubic hair appeared later than typical boys', and he constantly scrutinised his testicles on a daily basis, watching his buddies pass this milestone before him. "Pubes," as he dubbed them, were a recurring theme in his notebook. "Not enough pubes yet," he complained. "Years gone by. Ideals were obtained. Not yet created. Much after our pubes have stopped growing." In gym class, he would dress in a restroom stall rather than expose himself to the examination of the boys' locker room. When he was sixteen, pubes began to appear, albeit because of his light coloration, they were not as noticeable as those of other males.

Wendy began dating Pat O'Connor about the time Kurt turned seventeen. Wendy's age was O'Connor, and he made $52,000 as a longshoreman. Pat's pay was made public since he was the subject of one of Washington's first palimony cases shortly after he and Wendy became involved. It was filed by his ex-girlfriend, who claimed he ditched her for Wendy after convincing her to quit her job at the local nuclear power plant. It was a horrible case that lasted for the following two years. Pat identified his assets in court filings as a tiny residence, a few thousand dollars in savings, and a gun rack with three firearms—these guns, ironically, where to play a role in Kurt's career. Pat's ex-husband won $2500 in cash, a car, and her legal bills.

Pat spent the winter at Wendy's residence. Kurt grew to despise O'Connor, who was disliked by neither of Wendy's children. Kurt, like his real father and Franich, made Pat the topic of many of his songs and cartoons. And nearly from the start, Pat and Wendy had disputes that made Don and Wendy's fights look tame in comparison.

One specific outburst became one of the pillars of Kurt's personal musical mythos. Wendy went out seeking for Pat after a big fight and caught him "cheating on her," according to Kim. He was intoxicated, as usual." Wendy raced home in a passion, muttering about killing Pat. In a hurry, she had Kim collect Pat's guns and place them in a large plastic bag. Wendy declared she was going to murder Pat when he returned. Kurt stated that Wendy tried to shoot Pat but couldn't figure out how to load the gun; his sister does not recall that twist. Wendy and Kim dragged a bag of guns two blocks from their house to the banks of the Wishkah River after Pat left. Wendy continued telling herself, "Got to get rid of these or I'm going to end up killing him," as they dragged the guns over the ground. She tossed them into the lake.

Kurt questioned Kim about the placement of the guns while Pat and Wendy reunited the next morning. Kurt and two of his mates fished the firearms out with the help of his thirteen-year-old sister. Kurt would subsequently relate this story, claiming that he swapped the firearms for his first guitar, despite the fact that he had owned a guitar since he was fourteen. Kurt was never one to let the truth get in the way of a good story, and the yarn about pawning his stepfather's firearms for his first guitar was simply too wonderful to pass up. All of the aspects of how he intended to be viewed as an artist—someone who converted redneck swords into punk rock ploughshares—were contained in this single story. In reality, he pawned the pistols but used the cash to purchase a Fender Deluxe amp.

Wendy and Pat's "guns in the river" event was only one of many. Kurt's strategy for avoiding these fights-or becoming the topic of them, because Pat loved nothing more than lecturing Wendy on what she should do with her errant son-was to make a swift dash from the front door to his room. In this regard, he was typical of most teenagers, though his entrances and exits were frantic. When he wanted to come out for a home job, such as using the phone or raiding the kitchen, he tried to time his outings to avoid Pat. His room became his haven, and his description of a trip back home in his notebook a few years later was as emotional as it was physical:

Every time I return, it's the same déjà vu, total depression, total hatred, and grudges that would last months at a time, old Pee Chees with contents of drawings of rocker dudes playing guitar, monsters, and sayings on the cover like, "This Bud's for you," or "Get high," intricate sketchings of bongs, alterations of sexual puns on the happy tennis-playing girl. Look around you and you'll notice Iron Maiden posters with shredded and hole-filled edges, as well as nails in the walls where tractor helmets are still placed today. Dents on the table from playing a beer game called quarter bounce for five years. I look around and see all this fucking junk, and what reminds me the most about my worthless adolescent is that every time I enter the room, I run my finger across the ceiling and feel the sticky residue from a collection of pot and cigarette smoke.

His disagreements with the grownups in the family reached a boiling point in the spring of 1984. He despised Wendy for her weakness with men, much as he despised his father's desire to remarry. He despised Pat even more since the older man gave advice in a way that highlighted Kurt's shortcomings. The two males in the household also had opposing views on how women should be treated. "Pat was a womaniser," Kim pointed out, "but Kurt wasn't." Kurt was incredibly courteous of women, despite the fact that he didn't have many relationships. He was looking for someone with whom he might fall in love." Pat's lectures on how "a man had to be a man and act like a man" were never-ending. When Kurt failed to meet Pat's expectations, he was labeled "a faggot." On one particular Sunday in April 1984, Pat's epithets were particularly harsh: "Why don't you ever bring any girls home?"" he inquired of Kurt. "When I was your age, there were girls in and out of my bed all the time."

Kurt went to a party with this piece of masculine advice. He met Jackie Hagara there. When she and her companion decided to go, Kurt suggested they go to his house-perhaps he saw an opportunity to impress Pat. Nonetheless, he sneaked them upstairs without waking the elders. The girlfriend was inebriated and passed out on the twin bed in the playroom outside Kurt's bedroom. With her pal unable to walk, Kurt assured Jackie, "You can crash here."

Kurt's long-awaited moment had finally arrived. He had long wished to shed his adolescent sexual fantasies and tell his high-school peers that he was no longer a virgin (in fact, he had been lying about the topic for several years, like most males his age). He was famished for the feel of skin on skin growing up in a world where males were rarely touched save for the occasional smack on the back. He had chosen a willing compatriot in Jackie. Her constant boyfriend was in jail on the night she found herself in Kurt's bedroom, despite the fact that she was just fifteen. As they entered Kurt's room, she knew what was going to happen next. As Jackie recalls, there was a moment when they gazed at each other and lust filled the room with the force of an internal combustion engine starting up.

Kurt turned off the lights, the couple undressed, and they got into bed, holding each other. It would be Kurt's first hug of a fully naked girl, a moment he had long fantasised about, a moment he had pictured in many nights of adolescent masturbation on this very bed. Jackie started kissing him. The door swung open as soon as their tongues met, and in came Kurt's mother.

Wendy was not pleased at all to find her son in bed with a naked girl. She was also annoyed to witness another girl pass out in the corridor. "Get out! Get out!"" she screamed. She'd come upstairs to show Kurt the lightning-the notion that a massive storm was brewing had escaped the young lovers-only to find her son in bed with a girl. Wendy yelled as she marched down the stairs, "Get the fuck out of my house!Pat, for his part, remained nothing on the subject, knowing that any comments he made would upset Wendy even more. Kurt's sister Kim hurried in from the next room when she heard a disturbance. She noticed Kurt and Jackie putting shoes on a female who was unconscious. "What the hell is going on?"" Kim wondered. "We're leaving," Kurt announced to his sister. He and Jackie carried the other girl down the stairs and went outside into one of the year's worst storms.

As Kurt and his two companions began walking down First Street-the fresh air had revived the intoxicated friend—it began to drizzle, and though this appeared to be an ominous sign, Kurt would lose his virginity before the sun rose. He was visibly shivering already, his boiling hormones mingling with wrath, embarrassment, and terror. Dressing in front of Jackie while still having an erection had been humiliating. As with his experience with the disabled girl, passion and shame were equally powerful forces within him, hopelessly interwoven and perplexing.

They made their way to Jackie's friend's place. But as soon as they stepped in, so did Jackie's lover, who had just been released from jail. Jackie had told Kurt about her paramour's violent tendencies, so Kurt pretended to be the other girl's date to avoid a confrontation. Kurt and the girl ended up spending the night together after Hagara and her boyfriend left. It wasn't the best sex, as she later admitted to Jackie, but it was intercourse, and that was all that counted to Kurt. He'd finally passed through that door, the big vaginal barrier, and he wasn't living a sexual lie any longer.

Kurt set out early in the morning to walk around Aberdeen in the early morning light. The storm had passed, the birds were chirping, and the earth felt more alive. He walked around for hours, waiting for school to start, watching the sun rise, and wondering where his life was going.

5:

The Will of Instinct

Kurt roamed the streets of Aberdeen early on Monday morning, sniffing her sex on his fingertips. It was an incredible sensation for someone who was preoccupied with smell. He only had to rub his fingers in his own crotch to experience the act, and when he inhaled them, her scent was still there. Already, his mind was forgetting that his sexual introduction had been a near disaster, and he was making it into a triumph in his memory. He was no longer a virgin, regardless of the circumstances-crummy sex or not. Being a romantic at heart, he imagined that this first sexual contact was simply the beginning of many enjoyable romps with this girl; that it was the beginning of his adult sexual experience; a balm that he could rely on, like alcohol or marijuana, to enable him escape his lot. He snatched a flower from a yard on his way to Weatherwax. Jackie noticed Kurt meekly walking toward the smoker's shack outside the high school, holding a single red rose—she assumed it was for her, but Kurt gave it to the girl he had slept with, who was unimpressed. What Kurt didn't realise was that Jackie was the one who had a crush on him. The other girl, on the other hand, was humiliated by her indiscretion and much more so by the flower. It was a difficult lesson, and for someone as sensitive as Kurt, it added to his confusion about his desire for love and the complexities of adult sexuality.

There were more pressing issues after school, the first of which was finding a place to live. Buzz accompanied him to grab his belongings. As Kurt had rightly predicted, this argument with his mother was unlike the others; they arrived to find her still enraged. "His mom was just freaking out the entire time, telling him what a total fucking loser he was," she said. "All he kept saying was, 'OK, Mom.'" Okay.' She made it apparent that she didn't want him in the house at all." Kurt began his final mental and physical exodus from his family as he gathered his valuable guitar and amp and placed his clothes in a series of Hefty rubbish bags. There had been other flights, and his pattern of fleeing began immediately after the divorce, but the majority of those moves were his. He felt powerless this time, and he was terrified of how he would care for himself. He was seventeen, a junior in high school, and failing the majority of his subjects. He'd never worked, had no money, and had everything in four Hefty bags. He was certain he was leaving, but he had no idea where.

If his divorce was the first betrayal, and his father's remarriage was the second, this third betrayal would be equally significant. Wendy had had enough of him. She told her sisters she "didn't know what to do with Kurt anymore." Their squabbles were increasing her problems with Pat, whom she was planning to marry, and she couldn't afford to lose that connection, even if only for financial reasons. Kurt suspected, possibly accurately, that one of his parents was selecting a new partner above him. It was a marginalisation that would haunt him for the rest of his life: combined with his previous emotional traumas, the experience of being kicked out would be one he would return to repeatedly, never totally free of the trauma. It would be barely beneath the surface, a pain that would engulf the rest of his life in a sense of deprivation. There could never be enough money, attention, or, most importantly, love since he understood how quickly it all went away.

Seven years later, he'd create a song about it called "Something in the Way." The oblique lyrics left the "something" unexplained, but there was no doubt that he was what was in the way. The song implies that the vocalist lives beneath a bridge. When pressed, Kurt usually repeated the same narrative about being tossed out of the house, dropping out of school, and living under the Young Street Bridge. It would later become one of his cultural biographies' touchstones, one of his most potent pieces of myth-making, the one item of Kurt's history assured to appear in any one-paragraph summary of his life: This youngster was so despised that he lived under a bridge. It was a striking and dark image, rendered all the more potent when Nirvana became renowned and pictures of the bottom of the Young Street Bridge began to emerge in periodicals, its rank foetid character visible even in photographs. It appeared to be something a troll would live under, rather than a child. The bridge was only two blocks from his mother's house, a distance that, according to Kurt, no amount of love could bridge.

Kurt's telling of the "living under the bridge" narrative, like the "guns for guitars" myth before it, was significantly inflated. "He never lived under that bridge," Krist Novoselic, who met Kurt that year in school, said. "He stayed there, but you couldn't live on those muddy banks with the tides coming in and out." That was revisionism on his part." His sister agreed, saying, "He never lived under the bridge." It was a hotspot for all the area youngsters to consume marijuana, but that was it." Locals contend that if Kurt ever slept under any Aberdeen bridge, it would have been the Sixth Street Bridge, a much larger span a half mile away that stretches across a small canyon and is popular with Aberdeen's homeless. Even this situation is difficult to envision because Kurt was a world-class whiner; few whiners could endure an Aberdeen spring outside, where the weather is nothing short of a daily downpour. The bridge narrative, on the other hand, has relevance, if only because Kurt emphatically repeated it so many times. He must have started to believe it himself at some time.

Even Kurt's version of events pales in comparison to the genuine story of where he spent his days and nights during this time period. His trip began on Dale Crover's porch, where he slept curled up like a kitten in a cardboard refrigerator box. When his welcome in Aberdeen ran out, his cunning and wiliness did not fail him: there were numerous ancient apartment buildings with central heating in the halls, and this is where he would spend most nights. He'd sneak in late, pick a big hallway, unscrew the overhead light, stretch out his bedroll, sleep, and wake up before the residents started their day. It was a life best summed up by a line he'd compose in a song a few years later: "It amazes me, the will of instinct." His natural survival talents came in handy, and he had a strong will.

Kurt and another boy called Paul White would walk up the hill to Grays Harbor Community Hospital when everything else failed. They would sleep in the waiting room there. Kurt, the more adventurous or desperate of the two, would boldly stroll through the hospital cafeteria line and charge meals to fictitious room numbers. "There was a television in the waiting room, and we could watch that all day," she recalled. "People always thought we were waiting for a patient who was ill or dying, and they'd never question you when it concerned that." This was the true tale behind the emotional truth conveyed in "Something in the Way," and arguably the biggest irony of his life-Kurt had ended up back where he started, back in the hospital with the magnificent view of the harbour, back where he was born seventeen years before. Here he was, sleeping in the waiting room like a fugitive, smuggling rolls out of the cafeteria, pretending to be a bereaved relative of someone who was ill, but the only genuine ailment he felt in his heart was loneliness.

Kurt returned to live with his father after around four months on the streets. It wasn't easy for Kurt, and the fact that he'd consider moving back in with a parent demonstrates his desperation. Don and Jenny discovered Kurt sleeping on an old sofa in a garage across the alley from Wendy's house after hearing he was homeless. "He was very angry at everybody at that time, and he wanted everyone to think that nobody would take him, which was pretty much what was true," she said.

Kurt returned to his basement room in the Fleet Street house in Montesano. His power clashes with his father grew more heated—it was as if his time away from Don had just strengthened his resolve.

Kurt's presence there was no longer a temporary arrangement; they had mutually outgrown their need or desire for each other. Kurt's guitar made everything better, and he practised for hours. His friends and family began to realise he was getting better at it. "He could play any song after listening to it just once, anything from Air Supply to John Cougar Mellencamp," his stepbrother James recounted. Kurt and James watched This Is Spinal Tap five times in a row, and he quickly began to repeat dialogue from the film and play the band's songs.

While Kurt was reunited with Don and Jenny, another family member committed suicide. Kenneth Cobain, Leland's sole surviving brother, became depressed after his wife's death and shot himself in the head with a.22 calibre revolver. The loss was nearly too much for Leland to bear: the sad deaths of his father, son Michael, and three brothers tempered his bluster with deep depression. If Ernest's death is considered a suicide by drinking, then all three of Leland's brothers died by their own hand, two by shooting themselves.

Kurt wasn't close to these uncles, but there was a sorrowful pall over the house, as if the family had been cursed on all sides. Kurt's stepmother worked hard to find him a job doing lawn labour because that was the only work available in Monte besides logging. Kurt mowed a few lawns before becoming bored. He searched in the classifieds once or twice, but there weren't many work opportunities in Montesano. The county's largest commercial project, the Satsop Nuclear Power Plant, had gone bankrupt before it was completed, leaving unemployment at 15%, double the state average. Things came to a climax when Don said that if Kurt wasn't going to school or working, he had to join the military. Don invited a Navy recruiter to speak with his kid the following night.

Instead of a strong, headstrong guy who could have seized the Navy man by the collar and hurled him headfirst out the door later in life, the recruiter discovered a sad and broken youngster. To everyone's amazement, Kurt listened to the pitch. Kurt replied he'd think about it at the end of the evening, much to his father's relief. The service sounded like hell to Kurt, but it was hell with a different zip code. Kurt informed Jesse Reed, "At the very least, the Navy could give you three hots and a cot." The security of shelter and food without a parental fee to pay appeared appealing to a child who had been living on the streets and sleeping in hospital waiting rooms. When Don tried to persuade him to let the recruiter return the next night, Kurt said no way.

He found religion out of desperation. During 1984, he and Jesse had become inseparable, even attending church together. Jesse's parents, Ethel and Dave Reed, were born-again Christians who attended the Central Park Baptist Church, which was located halfway between Monte and Aberdeen. Kurt began to attend Sunday services on a regular basis and even attended the Wednesday night Christian Youth Group. He was baptised in the church that October, despite the fact that no members of his family were there. Kurt even had a born-again conversion experience, according to Jesse: "One night we were walking over the Chehalis River bridge and he stopped and said he accepted Jesus Christ into his life." He requested that God 'enter into his life.' I recall him mentioning the discoveries and peace that everyone talks about when they accept Christ." Kurt adopted the tone of an evangelical born-again Christian during the next few weeks. He started chastising Jesse for smoking marijuana, ignoring the Bible, and being a bad Christian. Kurt's religious conversion coincided with one of his many clean periods; his drug and alcohol history was always characterised by a binge followed by a fast. That month, he wrote a letter to his Aunt Mari in which he expressed his opinions on marijuana:

I just got done watching Reefer Madness on MTV...It was made in the thirties and if people took one toke of the devil drug, marijuana, they spaced-out big time, killed each other, had affairs, ran over innocent victims in cars. They sent this teenager, who looked like the Beaver, on a

murder rap. Wow, that's more excitement than I can handle. It was like a
big over-exaggeration. But I accept the whole idea behind it. Pot sucks. I
know that from personal experience, because for a while there I became
almost as lethargic as a mouldy piece of cheese. I think that was a big
problem with my mom and I.

Kurt shed his faith like a pair of outgrown jeans almost as soon as he mailed the letter and found himself relaxing into the pattern of church life. "He was hungry for it," he continued, "but it was a transitory moment out of fear." Kurt resumed consuming marijuana after his nervousness passed. He stayed at Central Park Baptist for another three months, but his sermon, according to Jesse, "was more moving against God." He went on an anti-God rampage after that."

Kurt injured his finger while washing dishes at work in March 1985 and quit in a panic. "He had to get stitches," I recall, "and he told me that if he lost his finger and couldn't play guitar, he'd kill himself." Kurt hid in his house because he had no employment and an injury that prevented him from playing the guitar. He persuaded Jesse to skip school, and the two of them planned to spend the entire day drinking or using drugs. "He withdrew more and more," Ethel Reed said. "We attempted to entice Kurt out, but we couldn't. As time passed, we realised that we weren't assisting him and that all we were doing was providing a safe haven for him to retreat from people."

Kurt's dissociation reached a climax in April, when he lost his key and kicked in a window to gain entry. The Reeds had had enough and informed Kurt he needed to find another place to live. It was a rainy April in Grays Harbor that year, and while most kids his age were worried about going to prom or preparing for graduation, Kurt was hunting for shelter once more.

Kurt was back on the streets, continuing the never-ending cycle of sleeping in friends' garages or crashing in hallways. Desperate, he eventually appealed to the government for help, obtaining $40 per month in food stamps. He obtained work at the YMCA beginning May 1 through the local unemployment office. He would consider this brief career as his favourite day job, despite the fact that it was part-time and funded by a local "Youth Work" grant. He had a glorified housekeeping job, but he was the substitute lifeguard or activity instructor when other staff were out ill. Kurt enjoyed his job, especially working with children. Kurt appreciated stepping in as a lifeguard despite not being a particularly great swimmer. Kevin Shillinger, who lived a street away from the YMCA, saw Kurt instructing five- and six-year-olds how to play T-ball—he was smiling the entire time. He could find the self-esteem he lacked in other parts of his life by working with children: he was good with them, and they were non-judgmental.

He also worked a second part-time job, which he rarely mentioned. It was a janitorial post at Weatherwax High School. Every evening, he would put on a brown jumpsuit and push a mop around the halls of the school from which he had dropped out. Though the school year was nearly over by the time he started, the disparity between his peers' college preparation and his own particulars left him feeling as low as he had ever felt in his life. He only lasted two months before giving up.

Jesse followed Kurt out of the Reeds' home. Jesse and his girlfriend stayed at Jesse's grandparents' house in Aberdeen for a bit. They then moved into an apartment at 404 North Michigan Street on June 1, 1985. This little $100-a-month studio-the walls of which were painted pink, earning it the nickname "the pink apart-ment"-was a dump by any standard, but it was their dump. They augmented the apartment's basic furnishings with lawn ornaments, Big Wheel tricycles, and backyard recliners stolen from the neighbourhood. Kurt used a picture window facing the street as his public easel, writing "666" and "Satan Rules" on the glass with soap. A shaving gel-covered blow-up doll hangs from a noose. Edge Shaving Gel was all over the place in the apartment; samples had been given out throughout the area, and Kurt and Jesse realised they could get high by sucking the fumes from the cans. They'd taken a couple of acid hits when a Grays Harbor County sheriff came on the door and told them to take the doll away. Fortunately, the officer did not enter their apartment, where he would have discovered three weeks' worth of dishes stacked in the sink, numerous pieces of stolen lawn furniture, Edge Shaving Gel wiped on all the walls, and the spoils of their most recent prank—stealing crosses from gravestones and painting them with polka dots.

During the summer of 1985, Kurt would have several run-ins with the law. Kurt, Jesse, and their friends would wait for nightfall like werewolves before terrorising the area by stealing lawn furniture or spray-painting buildings. Though Kurt subsequently claimed that his graffiti messages were political ("God is Gay," "Abort Christ," among other phrases), the majority of what he scribbled was nonsense. He outraged a boat-owning neighbour by spray-painting "Boat Ack" in red letters on the ship's hull; on the opposite side, he wrote, "Boat people go home." He painted graffiti on the YMCA's wall one night, and the next day, in a poetic stroke of justice, he was assigned the task of cleaning it off.

On the evening of July 23, 1985, Detective Michael Bens was patrolling Market Street, about a block from the Aberdeen Police Station, when he noticed three men and a young kid in an alley. As Benson's car arrived, the men ran, but the blond youngster stood frozen, like a deer in headlights, and Bens observed him drop a graffiti marker. On the wall behind him, there was a prophecy: "Ain't got no how watchamacallit." It was a work of art in typography, with the letters in random upper and lower case with every "T" four times larger than the other characters.

The child bolted and ran two blocks before being apprehended by the patrol car. He came to a halt and was handcuffed as a result. He introduced himself as "Kurt Donald Cobain," and he was the epitome of civility. He drafted and signed a statement at the station, which read in full:

Tonight, while standing behind SeaFirst Bank in the alley by the library talking to three other people, I wrote on the SeaFirst building. I don't know why I did it, but I did. What I put on the wall was, "Ain't got no how watchamacallit." Now I see how silly it was for me to have done this, and I'm sorry that I did. When the police car came into the alley I saw him, and I dropped the red marker that I had used.

He was fingerprinted, mug photographs were taken, and he was freed, but he was compelled to appear in court for a hearing a few weeks later. He was fined $180, given a 30-day suspended sentence, and advised not to get into any further trouble.

That was easier said than done for Kurt, an eighteen-year-old. When Jesse was at work one night, the typical "Cling-Ons" showed up and everyone jammed on their guitars. A tall man with a moustache, one of the neighbours, beat on the wall and told them to be quiet. Kurt later told this story, claiming that the neighbour savagely beat him for hours. It was one of several stories Kurt shared about how he was often abused by Aberdeen's rednecks. "It wasn't like that," Steve Shillinger recalled. "The guy did come over, told him to be quiet, and when Kurt wised off, the fellow punched him a couple of times and told him to 'shut the fuck up.'" Jesse wasn't present that night, but in all his years knowing Kurt, he only recalls one fight: "He was usually too busy making people laugh." I was constantly nearby to shield him." Jesse, like Kurt, was short, but he had lifted weights and was strongly built.

Jesse definitely would have killed for Kurt during the pink apartment time, which Kurt took full advantage of. Kurt stated one day that they were both getting Mohawks. They marched down to the Shillingers, produced hair clippers, and Jesse soon had a Mohawk. Kurt declared that shaving was a bad idea when the time arrived.

"One time, Kurt said if he could write something on my forehead, I could write something on his," Jesse added. "He took permanent ink and wrote '666' on me, then ran away." Everyone used to experiment on me since I was a nitwit. They would always encourage me to test a drug or a drink first." Kurt's torment of his best friend had a nasty side. Despite his misbehaviour, Jesse had graduated that spring. Kurt stole images from Jesse's yearbook, plastered them to the wall, and crossed red crosses across them one night while Jesse was working at Burger King. It was more a manifestation of his own self-hatred than a reflection of his love for Jesse. Kurt may have kicked Jesse out of the apartment out of embarrassment over his rage. Never mind that Jesse was the one who had made the deposit. Jesse soon moved home with his grandma, and Kurt was on his own. Jesse had already decided to join the Navy, which made Kurt feel intimidated. It was a pattern he would repeat throughout his life: rather than losing someone he cared about, he would retreat first, generally by inventing some phoney argument to reduce the abandonment he thought was unavoidable.

While residing in the pink apartment, Kurt continued to write songs, many of which were hilarious, despite the fact that they were still thinly disguised stories about the individuals and events around him. That summer, he wrote "Spam," a song against the meat product, and "The Class of 85," an attack on Jesse and the graduation class he missed. It went something like this: "We are all the same, just flies on a turd." Even though his lyrics were about a small world, Kurt was thinking big. "I'm going to make a record that's going to be even bigger than U2 or R.E.M.," he boasted to Steve Shillinger. Kurt adored both of these bands, and he never stopped bragging about how fantastic the Smithereens were, but he was cautious not to mention them around Buzz for fear of breaking the punk code that no commercial music mattered. He read every fanzine or music journal he could get his hands on, which wasn't many in Aberdeen; he even typed out lengthy fictitious interviews with himself for nonexistent publications. Kurt and Steve discussed launching their own fanzine, even going so far as to produce a sample issue; Steve abandoned the project when he discovered Kurt was writing good reviews of songs he had never heard. Kurt also mentioned launching his own record company, and one night he and Steve recorded a spoken word monologue by a guy named Scotty Karate. Nothing came of it, as with so many of his ideas at the time.

There was no money for fanzines or record labels, and even paying the rent was difficult. Kurt was evicted two months after Jesse left. When Kurt wasn't home, his landlord arrived at the apartment, boxed up his meagre items, including the stolen crosses and Big Wheels, and put them on the street.

Kurt was homeless for the third time in two years. He pondered the Navy once more. Trevor Briggs was enlisting, and he encouraged Kurt to take advantage of the Navy's buddy system, which allowed them to be placed in boot camp together. Grays Harbor's unemployment rate had risen even higher, and choices for an eighteen-year-old dropout were limited. Kurt proceeded to the Navy recruiting headquarters on State Street and took the ASVAB occupational aptitude test for three hours. He passed, and the Navy agreed to take him; subsequently, Kurt said he achieved the best score ever recorded on the test, although this was difficult to believe given that the test included maths. Kurt refused to join at the last minute, as he has previously.

Kurt slept most nights in the backseat of Greg Hokanson's mother's beat-up Volvo vehicle, dubbed "the vulva." By the time October arrived around and the weather turned terrible, nights in the car seat were unpleasant. Kurt quickly found a new patron in the Shillinger family, who consented to take him in after much pleading from Kurt.

Lamont Shillinger taught English at Weatherwax and, like Dave Reed, came from a pious family. Despite having left the Mormon religion years ago, Lamont continued to strive to be, as he put it, "a freelance decent human being." Other similarities were the Shillingers eating supper together, spending time as a family, and encouraging their sons to play music. Kurt was welcomed as family and assigned responsibilities, which he completed without complaint, glad for the opportunity. Kurt slept on a sofa in the living room, storing his sleeping bag behind it during the day, because space was limited in the Shillinger household (they had six children of their own). In 1985, he spent Thanksgiving and Christmas morning with the Shillingers. Kurt got a much-needed new pair of Levi's from Lamont. Kurt went to Wendy's house later that day; she had just given birth to his half-sister Brianne. The new infant brightened the O'Connor household, but there was no discussion of Kurt returning.

6:

Didn't Love Him Enough

On September 1, 1986, Wendy loaned Kurt $200, which was enough for a deposit and the first month's rent, and Kurt moved into his first "house." That legal description of the structure at 100012 East Second Street in Aberdeen was far too generous; it was a shack that would have been condemned as uninhabitable under any reasonable building code in many other municipalities. The roof was rotting, the front porch boards had collapsed, and there was no refrigerator or stove. The layout was oddly divided into five small rooms: two living areas, two bedrooms, and a single bathroom. It was hidden behind another property, hence the unusual address. Nonetheless, the location-two blocks from his mother's house-was excellent for a nineteen-year-old who was still under Wendy's psychic control. In the previous year, their connection had improved. With Kurt gone, they grew closer emotionally; he still craved Wendy's admiration and attention, despite masking his sensitivity. She would bring him meals on occasion, and he could go to her house to wash laundry, use the phone, or loot the refrigerator as long as his stepfather was not present. The shanty was behind a grocery shop and close to the Salvation Army. Kurt kept beer in an icebox on the back porch because the house didn't have a refrigerator until the neighbour's kids discovered it.

Kurt chose Matt Lukin from the Melvins as his roommate. Kurt had always wanted to be Melvin, and living with Lukin was the closest he could get. Kurt's main addition to the house was placing a bathtub full of turtles in the middle of the living room and drilling a hole in the floor to allow the turtle effluence to run beneath the floorboards. Lukin, on the other hand, attempted to restructure the walls using his carpentry talents. Lukin was also 21, which meant he could buy beer. The Fat Man will soon fade into obscurity.

It was a party house and, later, a band house. Buzz Osborne and Dale Crover visited frequently with Lukin as a roommate, and because the living room was loaded with band gear, there were impromptu jams. A motley band of Melvins' "Cling-Ons" moved into the hut. Despite the fact that much of the bonding was based on the objective of inebriation, Kurt's time in 100012 East Second was the most social of his life. Kurt even made acquaintances with the neighbours, or at least their teenage children, who were foetal alcohol syndrome victims-but that didn't stop him from giving them beer. Another neighbour, a senile senior citizen dubbed "Lynyrd Skynyrd hippie," would come by every day to drum along to Kurt's copy of Lynyrd Skynyrd's Greatest Hits.

Kurt found a job as a maintenance man at the adjacent Polynesian Condominium Resort to help pay the rent. He'd ride the bus the 25 miles to the coastal resort. It was a simple job because his main role was to maintain things, and the 66-room resort was in good condition. When a position as a maid became available, he suggested Krist's girlfriend, Shelli. "He used to sleep on the bus," she said. "It was funny because he wasn't even a maintenance man." He'd sleep in the motel rooms or raid the freezers in the rooms after people left." Aside from the $4-an-hour starting compensation, one advantage of the job was that he simply had to wear a brown work shirt, rather than the dreaded uniform.

He braggingly described the job to his buddies as "maintenance butt-boy" and how he could spend most of his days sneaking into rooms and watching television, but what he didn't tell anyone was that he also had to clean rooms on occasion. Kurt Cobain had to work as a maid because he was such a lousy housekeeper that he should be in some type of hall of fame. Kurt would fantasise about a future other than cleaning toilets and making beds on the bus to the resort every morning, usually drunk over.

What he did think about all the time was starting a band. It was a continual nagging thought in his thoughts, and he spent hours trying to figure out how it might be done. Buzz had done it, and if Buzz could do it, he was confident he could as well. On a dozen occasions in 1987, he travelled as a roadie with the Melvins to performances in Olympia, a college town an hour east, where he saw an enthusiastic, albeit small, punk rock audience. He'd made it all the way to Seattle with the band, and while it meant schlepping equipment and going to work the next morning with no sleep, it was a taste of a bigger world. Being a Melvins roadie was hardly a glamorous job: there was no money or groupies, and Buzz was notorious for treating everyone as if they were servants. But it was an abuse Kurt readily tolerated because nothing escaped his scrutiny. Kurt was growing in confidence, especially when it came to his guitar playing; while he carried Buzz's amp, he imagined the roles were reversed. He practised whenever he could, and the fact that he was improving was one of the few sources of self-assurance he could find. His wishes were realised when Buzz and Dale invited him to jam with them in Olympia on the last night of Gessco. Despite the fact that only approximately twenty people attended the show-the poster labelled them as Brown Towel, when their name was supposed to be Brown Cow-it was his first performance in front of a paid audience. Instead of playing guitar, Kurt read poetry while Buzz and Dale thrashed at theirs.

Many of his self-destructive tendencies from the pink flat were still present at the hut. Tracy Marander, who met him during this time, said he ingested a significant amount of LSD. "Kurt was doing a lot of acid, sometimes five times a week," she said. At least part of the rationale for his increased drug use was, oddly, union devotion; at the time, an Aberdeen supermarket strike meant you had to drive to Olympia to get beer or cross a picket line, and Kurt's normal choice was to take acid instead. When he did buy beer, it was usually "Animal Beer," so named because Schmidt's cans featured nature scenes. Kurt would splurge on Rolling Rock when he had more money because, as he told his buddies, "it's almost like 'rock 'n' roll' spelled backwards."

Kurt's shack year was one of his longest and most extreme drug-abusing times. Previously, he had a pattern of bingeing and then drying up, but at the shack, he loved getting screwed up like he enjoyed little else. "He was always pushing it," Steve Shillinger recalled, "using just a little bit more than anyone else, and taking more as soon as he was no longer high." When he ran out of money for pot, acid, or beer, he'd revert to huffing aerosol cans. "He was really into getting fucked up; drugs, acid, any kind of drug," Novoselic pointed out. "In the middle of the day, he'd get hammered." He was a shambles."

He also continued to talk about suicide and dying young. Ryan Aigner lived one block away and recalls regular chats about death from the minute he met Kurt. "What are you going to do when you're thirty?" Ryan once asked Kurt." "I'm not concerned about what will happen when I'm thirty," Kurt said, in the same tone he would use to describe a faulty spark plug, "since I'm never going to make it to thirty." "You know what life is like after thirty—I don't want that." The thought was so strange to Ryan, who saw the world with a young man's sense of possibility, that he was silent for a moment. Ryan could sense Kurt's anguish: "He was the shape of suicide." He dressed like suicide, walked like suicide, and talked like suicide."

Kurt had left the resort job by late April. In order to make ends meet, he would occasionally work as a carpet installer alongside Ryan. Kurt was liked by the carpet company's bosses, and Ryan informed him that a full-time employment was feasible. But Kurt was put off by the thought of heavy work, and he was frightened of damaging his guitar-playing hand on the double-edged knives needed to cut the carpet. "These hands are far too important to me," Kurt contended. "I could ruin my guitar-playing career," he claimed, adding that if he sliced his hands and was unable to play, he would die.

Kurt's choice of the word "career" to describe his music demonstrates the one location where hope existed. Those long hours of practice were beginning to pay off. He was writing songs at a breakneck pace, hastily scribbling out the lyrics on notepad sheets. You could practically see his brain piecing together a plan as he was learning so quickly and absorbing so much from the things he saw and recordings he listened to. There wasn't much emphasis on "the band," because there was no such thing at the time; instead, caught up in his desire to compose music, he arranged three or four ensembles at the same time. Kurt on guitar, Krist on bass, and a local drummer named Bob McFadden were among the first bands to practise in the shack. Kurt was on drums, Krist was on guitar, and Steve "Instant" Newman was on bass in another. To call these groups "groups," as Kurt subsequently did, was a bit of an exaggeration: they were only real in Kurt's mind, and he would put them together in the same manner that someone could construct the perfect fantasy baseball team. After noticing that the Melvins had been paid $60 for a job one night, Kurt and Krist established the Sellouts, a band that only rehearsed Creedence Clearwater Revival songs, believing that they would go over well in Aberdeen bars. Kurt talked about these bands as if they had long careers, even though most of them only played rehearsals. Only one outfit, the Stiff Woodies, was put on exhibit in public, during a kegger of high-school youngsters who disregarded them.

While the jam sessions and parties kept Kurt busy, by the beginning of 1987, he was becoming dissatisfied with Aberdeen. While his pals were delighted to listen to music for pleasure on Friday nights, Kurt was practising a guitar riff or creating a song on Saturday morning. All he needed was a vehicle to express his artistic vision, and that was about to change. He and Krist formed an unnamed band with a neighbour drummer called Aaron Burckhard; Krist played bass, Burckhard drummed, and Kurt sang and played guitar. It was the birth of Nirvana and Kurt's first foray into being a musical alpha male. During the first few months of 1986, they practised practically every night until Kurt felt they had done enough for the evening. They would drive to Kentucky Fried Chicken after rehearsal. "Kurt loved Chicken Littles from KFC," Burckhard recalled. "Once, Kurt took electrical tape and made an inverted cross on the drive-thru speaker." We laughed our asses off in the van while the personnel had to come outside to pull it off."

Buzz revealed in early spring that he was heading to California and that the Melvins were disbanding. It was a watershed moment in Aberdeen band history, and Kurt must have thought he saw a Judas in his midst while witnessing it. "What happened," Lukin recalled, "was that I got left behind." The band was allegedly disbanded, which was just a ruse to get me out. 'Oh, no, I'm not even going to be in a band,' Buzz said. I'm just relocating to California.' But a month later, they were back on the road as the Melvins. It was difficult since it was the same way Buzz had me kick out our former drummer."

The separation of his roommate from the Melvins would be a watershed moment in Kurt's life: everyone took sides in this feud, and Kurt dared to oppose Buzz for the first time. "Kurt drifted away from the Melvins creatively and emotionally that day," Ryan said. " Kurt could immediately tell that his own pop-influenced songs would never live up to Buzz's high standards. Though he still talked about his affection for the Melvins, he had outgrown Buzz as a role model. It was a necessary step if he was to find his own voice, and while it was difficult, it emancipated him creatively and provided him artistic space.

Kurt and Lukin had also gotten irritated with each other—Kurt disliked a couple of Lukin's pals. He took masking tape and ran it down the centre of the house, telling Lukin and his buddies they had to stay on their side in a manoeuvre straight out of a "I Love Lucy" episode. When one of Lukin's friends grumbled about having to cross the tape to use the restroom, Kurt said, "Go to the bathroom out in the yard, because the bathroom is on my side." Lukin left. Kurt went without a roommate for a long time until a friend from Olympia, Dylan Carlson, came in. Dylan resembled Brian Wilson of the Beach Boys during his lost years, with long, brown hair and a scruffy beard, but what came out of his mouth were outlandish opinions on religion, racism, and politics. Dylan was a character, yet he was clever, creative, and nice, all of which Kurt valued. They had met at the Brown Cow event and struck up a friendship. Dylan relocated to Aberdeen, reportedly to work as a carpet installer with Kurt. The employment was hardly ideal: "Our boss was this total drunk," Dylan recounted. "When we arrived at work in the morning, he passed out on the office floor. "One time, he was passed out in front of the door, and we couldn't get in to get him up." The jobs broke apart, but Dylan and Kurt's friendship endured. Kurt welcomed 1987 and his twentieth year with a new band, a new best buddy, and some amazing tunes. Surprisingly, his sexual life would soon grow when Tracy Marander became his girlfriend. They became friends because both Kurt and Tracy owned pet rats. He had met her two years earlier outside a punk club in Seattle, which had also been the site of one of his drinking arrests. Kurt and Buzz were drinking in a car when Tracy came by to say hello, and he was so engrossed that he didn't notice a police cruiser pulling up. eventually kept running into each other throughout the next year, and eventually married in early 1987. "I had been flirting with him for quite a while," Tracy told me. "I think he had a hard time believing a girl actually liked him."

Tracy was the ideal girlfriend for Kurt, who was twenty years old, and she would be a significant milestone in his journey toward adulthood. She was a year older, had gone to hundreds of punk rock shows, and understood a lot about music, which was a tremendous sexual turn-on for Kurt. She was a down-to-earth beauty with dark hair, a curvaceous physique, and wide eyes that were as brilliantly brown as his were blue. Everyone she encountered became a friend; in this, and many other ways, she couldn't have been more dissimilar to him. He fell in love with her right away, despite the fact that he never believed he deserved her. These deep traumas and his propensity of disengagement manifested themselves early in their relationship. Tracy couldn't have said anything more painful the first time they went to bed together, as they lay in the afterglow of sex, when she observed, seeing him naked, "God, you are so skinny." Kurt's reaction was to change his clothes and storm outside. He did, however, return.

Tracy resolved to love him so much that his fear would go; she would love him so much that he would even be able to love himself. But for Kurt, this was dangerous territory, with an excuse for self-doubt and anxiety lurking around every turn. That spring, the only thing he cared for more than Tracy was his pet rat, Kitty. He had nurtured the male rat from birth, initially feeding him with an eyedropper. The rat was normally kept in his cage, but on rare occasions, Kurt would let it run around the home because a few rat turds wouldn't ruin the dirty carpet. Kurt saw a spider on the ceiling and persuaded Kitty to get it one day while Kitty was racing around the hut. "'See that fucker, Kitty?'" 'Get him, kill him, get him, kill him, get him, kill him,' Kurt wrote in his journal. But Kitty was unable to tackle the spider, and when Kurt returned with a can of Brut deodorant spray to destroy it, he heard a sorrowful scream and peered down to see: *My left foot...on top of the skull of my rat. He squealed and bled as he leaped around. "I'm sorry," I screamed approximately 30 times. I picked him up in his soiled underwear. Put him in a bag, found a two-by-four piece of wood, carried him outside, clubbed him, laid it on its side, and trod all over the sack. I could feel his bones and organs collapsing. It took approximately two minutes to put him out of his torment, and then I spent the rest of the night in misery. I clearly didn't love him as much as I do today. I returned to the bedroom and examined the blood smears and spider. I screamed, "Fuck you," to him and considered killing him, but instead left him to crawl across my face while I lay awake all night.*

7:

Soupy Sales in My Fly

Kurt Cobain's career as a bandleader was nearly finished before it started. On a stormy night in early March 1987, the band finally drove out of Aberdeen in a panel van loaded with equipment, bound for their debut gig. Kurt had spent countless hours considering various names for the band, including Poo Poo Box, Designer Drugs, Whisker Biscuit, Spina Biffida, Cut Bomb, Egg Flog, Pukeaharrea, Puking Worms, Fish Food, Bat Guano, and the Incompetent Fools (intentionally misspelt). But, as of March 1987, he hadn't decided on one.

They were on their way to Raymond, a half-hour south of Aberdeen but more like Aberdeen than Aberdeen itself; it was a town of loggers and rednecks, with practically every employment involving timber. Choosing Raymond for their first play was akin to a Broadway production debuting in the Catskills—it was an opportunity to test things out on a less discerning or sophisticated audience.

Ryan Aigner, who had been their manager for a brief while due to his outgoing personality, had arranged the gig. He nagged Kurt to perform in public, and when his friend refused, Ryan booked a gig at a party without Kurt's permission. Ryan got a carpet van from his employer, loaded up their equipment, and gathered Kurt, Krist, Burckhard, Shelli, and Tracy, who were forced to sit among rolls of carpet. Throughout the drive, Kurt bemoaned that the band, which had yet to play anyplace other than his modest cabin, deserved something better than this unpaid job. "We're playing in Raymond," he remarked, as if the town's name were an insult. "And at someone's house, no less." They haven't even heard of radio yet. They're going to despise us." "Kurt's theory," Ryan observed, "was that the audience would either hate them, which they would embrace, or the audience would love them, which would also be fine." "He was prepared for either." This was a classic example of a technique Kurt would use for the remainder of his career: He felt he could insulate himself from actual failure by downplaying victory and, in fact, announcing the worst possible case. If the actual occurrence he dreaded was anything less than a total calamity, he could declare some measure of triumph in having once again outwitted fate. This time, however, his prediction would come true.

The house was located at 17 Nussbaum Road, seven miles outside of Raymond in the middle of a field, up a gravel road. Kurt was terrified when they arrived at 9:30 p.m. and saw an audience of teenagers he didn't know. "When I saw what the band looked like," Vail Stephens, who was at the party, recalled, "I said, 'Uh oh.'" They didn't resemble the people we hung around with." Kurt had the same notion as he looked about at the dozen kids wearing Led Zeppelin T-shirts and sporting mullet haircuts. Krist was barefoot, while Kurt was dressed in a Munsters T-shirt and a metal stud bracelet with prongs that may have been purchased on London's King's Road in 1978.

They entered a residence decorated with a "Ernest" poster, a Metallica album flat, and a Def Leppard album poster. Several stolen street signs, including a "Mile 69" highway marker, were nailed to a beam. A Tama drum kit, as well as a Marshall stack, were permanently installed in one corner of the small living room, and there was a keg outside the kitchen.

It took some time for the band to set up their equipment, and during that time, the newcomers didn't exactly endear themselves to their hosts. "He didn't say anything," Kim Maden stated of Kurt. "He had his hair down, it was kind of greasy, and it was in his face." Kurt, at least, was unlike Krist, who marched into the restroom and began peeing despite the fact that it was already occupied by a girl. Krist entered the medicine cabinet, found a container of fake Halloween blood, which he used to cover his nude chest, found some duct tape to wrap over his nipples, and began rummaging through the prescription medication. He exited the restroom, ignoring the keg, and headed to the refrigerator, where he saw Michelob Light and exclaimed, "Hey, there's good beer!" Kurt had started playing at that point, and Krist had to dash to collect his bass because Nirvana's first show had begun.

They started with "Downer," one of Kurt's first tracks. It listed classic Cobain laments about the plight of humanity. "Hand out lobotomies / To save little families," Kurt Cobain crooned. The sombre lyrics were utterly missed on the Raymond audience, who could only hear the meaty guitar and bass riffs. Kurt raced through it, despite the fact that the song and others that followed were quite competent. It was all there, every bit of the Nirvana that would conquer the world in the years to come, by their very first public show: the tone, the attitude, the frenzy, the slightly off-kilter rhythms, the remarkably melodic guitar chords, the driving bass lines that were guaranteed to move your body, and, most importantly, Kurt's hypnotic focus. He wasn't yet a fully fledged performer-in fact, no one at the party recalls him ever raising his head or pulling his hair out of his face-but all the basic, fundamental building blocks were there. He was worth seeing just because he seemed so focused.

The audience didn't notice because they were doing what every group of teens at a party does: drinking and socialising. The fact that the audience did not applaud after they finished their first song was by far the most astonishing aspect of the show. Krist was the only one who sounded excited, saying, "That sounds pretty good from here," maybe to keep Kurt's edgy ego from splitting. Ryan, who was drunk, responded, "It sounds a hell of a lot better than usual." "I think you guys might buy a decent P.A.," Kurt said after concluding his first original song in front of an audience. "We do have a decent P.A.," Tony Poukkula, who resided in the house, contended, "it just keeps blowing up." Shelli yelled at Krist to keep his pants on because they were the only clothes he had left, while Kurt remarked, "There's a Soupy Sales in my fly." "Beastie Boys," one woman exclaimed. "Bestiality Boys," Kurt explained.

Kurt noticed Poukkula, a hot guitar player in the region, putting on his Fender and approaching the band as they tuned between songs. What Ryan hadn't informed Kurt was that Poukkula had portrayed the event as a jam session. Kurt's reaction was one of terror, as he did not want to share the spotlight even at this early stage in his career. "That'd be cool to jam," Kurt deceivingly said to Tony, "but do you mind if we play through our set?" I don't know any peppy tunes, and it's fine to improvise, but I only do it when I'm drunk—that way I don't care." Poukkula agreed and sat down. Kurt was next called upon to entertain the audience, and neither Burckhard nor Krist, who was now sleeping on top of the console television, appeared to be prepared. "Let's just hit this one," Kurt said hurriedly. "Let's just figure out how we are going to play it." And with that, he launched into the opening guitar solo to "Aero Zeppelin," expecting his bandmates to join in, which they did. Once the song got rolling, it sounded as finished as it would when they recorded it a year later.

The people became restless as "Aero Zeppelin" came to an end. There was no applause this time, and Kurt was heckled, though to be fair, much of the heckling came from Krist and Ryan, who were both so drunk they couldn't stand. The band had managed to pacify the crowd through volume during the songs, as they had done at many of their early gigs; they would not be so lucky during the song breaks.

Krist screamed, "Hey, who's got all the pot?"

"Acid. "I want acid!" exclaimed Shelli.

"You should just drink alcohol," a Raymond woman suggested.

"All I want is some good pot," Krist replied.

"I'm going to pot you in about five minutes," Ryan said. "Show some covers. Play whatever you want. I'm sick of you folks being stupid and retarded. "You're a moron."

"Let's play 'Heartbreaker,'" Krist exclaimed as he struck the introductory bass riff.

"Are you guys drunk?" a man inquired.

"Play it like Zeppelin did," another man exclaimed.

"Play it like Tony Iommi," another man urged.

"Do some Black Sabbath," yelled someone from the kitchen.

And then it almost went apart; Kurt was on the verge of shattering. Krist kept yelling, "play 'Heartbreaker,'" to which Kurt replied, "I don't know." Nonetheless, they started into the Zeppelin song, and Kurt's guitar performance was excellent. Kurt's rendition fell apart halfway through when he lost the lyrics, but the audience pushed him back, chanting "Solo." He performed his best Jimmy Page impersonation on "Heartbreaker," and incorporated sections of "How Many More Times," but there was no applause at the conclusion. Kurt wisely exclaimed, "'Mexican Seafood,' everybody," and they launched into this classic.

They then performed "Pen Cap Chew" and "Hairspray Queen." Krist was standing on top of the television by the end of this piece, doing a Kiss imitation with his tongue. Krist jumped out a window of the house while Kurt and Aaron continued to play. He returned to the home, looking like a three-year-old running through a sprinkler on a hot summer day, and then did it all again. "It was wild," Krist recalled. "Rather than just performing the show, we thought, why not host an event?" It was a big deal.'

What happened next ensured that the celebration will be remembered. Shelli and Tracy decided to add to the freak show by kissing each other and rubbing their hands over Krist's chest. Kurt presented the following song quickly: "This one's called 'Breaking the Law.'" They performed "Spank Thru," a song about masturbation that would later be titled. The Raymond audience may not have been the most sophisticated, but they began to suspect that they were the punchline to some sort of joke.

Shelli had the misfortune of hooking her necklace on the refrigerator door while attempting to steal some of the prized Michelob. A struggle broke out when Vail Stephens shut the door and shattered the necklace. "You fat, fucking cunt," Shelli cried at Vail as they fought in the driveway. "We were just being obnoxious on purpose," Shelli recalled. "To us they were rednecks, and we didn't want to be rednecks."

Kurt, seeing his first gig devolve into pandemonium, laid down his guitar and walked outside, amused and disgusted. Outside the house, an attractive young woman approached Kurt, and as she neared, he must have realised that his childhood fantasies of being a rock star and attracting groupies were now coming true. Instead of becoming a fan, this big-haired blond lady wanted to hear the lyrics to "Hairspray Queen." She apparently assumed the song was composed about her, possibly on the spot. It would be the first of many times Kurt's lyrics would be misconstrued. Even at his first performance, Kurt was irritated when the audience misinterpreted his actual intentions. "I'll tell ya the lyrics," he said, seeming offended. "They are, 'fuck, cunt, cocksucker, asshole, shit-eating, son-of-a-bitch, anal prober, mother fucker....'" The young lady stormed away.

Kurt went looking for Krist and discovered him urinating on the automobiles of the other guests atop the panel van. Kurt, seeing this exhibition and always wisely concerned with his own self-preservation, informed everyone that it was time to leave. They gathered their belongings and went, expecting their departure to be blocked by their hosts' fists and boots. Despite all the chaos and insults, and despite being stereotyped as rednecks, the Raymond crowd turned out to be more accepting than many of the audiences who would pay to see Nirvana over the next several years. Some had even said, "You guys aren't half bad." Hearing such remarks was like drinking an elixir for Kurt. Seeing his reflection in an audience, even if it wasn't entirely enthusiastic, was far more appealing than his own relentless self-criticism. It would have been a victory if the audience had done anything less than hang him from the nearest light post. The audience, distracted by cat fights, beer brawls, and a half-naked man jumping out of windows, had given him a brief taste of the opiate of attention, which he craved more than anything else in life.

As they crammed into the vehicle, there was some debate about who was the least drunk, and although Kurt was the most sober, no one trusted him to drive. He sat in the back as Burckhard drove. "Everybody went out to the driveway to watch them drive away," Jeff Franks, who lived in the house, remembered. "They were all sitting on the rolls of carpet in the back of the van, with the back door still open." We could see them lowering the slider as they raced away, gravel spewing from their tires."

There were no windows inside the vehicle, and with the sliding door closed, it was completely dark. They wouldn't play in front of an audience for several months, but they were already looking ahead, with a small portion of their legend already constructed.

8:

In High School Again

Kurt took another important voyage two months after the show in Raymond: he left Aberdeen for good. He had spent the first twenty years of his life there, but now that he had gone, he would rarely return. He piled his belongings, which at the time consisted of a Hefty bag of clothes, a crate of albums, and his now-empty rat cage, into Tracy's car for the 65-mile drive to Olympia. Olympia was a college town, the state capital, and one of the weirdest places west of the East Village, with a strange collection of punk rockers, artists, would-be-revolutionaries, feminists, and just plain weirdos. Students at Evergreen State College, colloquially known as "Greeners," developed their own curriculum. Kurt had no intention of attending college, but he was of the perfect age to blend in. He was to have a tumultuous connection with the town's artsy set-he sought for their approval while frequently feeling inadequate. It has been a recurring motif throughout his life. Kurt came to Olympia to live with Tracy in a studio apartment at 11412 Pear Street, an ancient house converted to a three-plex. It was little, but the rent, including utilities, was only $137.50 a month. And the location, just a few blocks from downtown, was excellent for Kurt, who didn't always have access to a working automobile. For the first month, he looked for work but had little success, while Tracy supported him by working in the Boeing aeroplane plant cafeteria in Seattle. She worked a graveyard shift, and because of the long trip, she left for work at ten o'clock at night and didn't get home until nine a.m. The work provided a consistent income, which they both knew Kurt couldn't supply, and she could steal food to boost her salary. Tracy began leaving Kurt "to do" lists because of her strange hours, and this method of communication became a ritual of their relationship. Kurt: sweep kitchen, behind cat litter box, rubbish can, under cat food," she wrote in late 1987. Shake the mats, put dirty dishes in the sink, clean up the corner, sweep the floor, shake the mats, vacuum, and clean the front room. Thank you very much." A heart and a happy face were used to sign the note. Kurt's reply: "Please set the alarm for 11 a.m." Then I'll do the dishes. Okay?" Kurt initially assisted with housekeeping, cleaning the dishes and even mopping the floor on occasion. Despite its small size, the flat required continuous cleaning due to their assortment of dogs. They possessed five cats, four rats, a cockatiel, two bunnies, and Kurt's turtles, and the actual inventory would vary over the following two years based on life span. The flat had an unfavourable odour that visitors frequently compared to a pet shop, but it was a home of sorts. Kurt gave their bunny the name Stew.

In addition, he painted the bathroom blood crimson and scribbled "REDRUM" on the wall, a reference to Stephen King's "The Shining." Because Kurt liked to write on walls, they cleverly covered most of them with rock posters, many of which were turned upside down, so he would have more area to draw. The few posters shown facing up had all been altered in some fashion. A massive Beatles poster now featured Paul McCartney with an afro and glasses. Kurt had added the following prose to a Led Zeppelin poster above the bed: "Loser, wino, alcoholic, scum, trash, degenerate, head lice, scabs, infections, pneumonia, diarrhoea, vomits blood, urine, malfunctioning bowel muscle, arthritis, gangrene, psychotic mental illness, unable to form sentences, expected to fend for himself in a box in the snow." A caricature of Iggy Pop and a depiction of a bottle of Thunderbird fortified wine were next to this screed. A picture collage he made of images of meat mingled with outdated medical depictions of sick vaginas adorned the refrigerator. "He was fascinated by things that were gross," Tracy said. And, despite the fact that Kurt rarely discussed religion-"I think he believed in God, but more in the devil than in God," Tracy said—there were crosses and other religious artefacts on the walls. Kurt adored snatching Virgin Mary figurines from the graveyard and drawing blood tears under her eyes. Tracy was raised Lutheran, and much of their religious debates focused on whether God could exist in such a horrific world, with Kurt arguing that Satan was stronger.

Kurt obtained a short-term $4.75-an-hour work at Lemons Janitorial Service, a small family-run cleaning service, after a few months of being a househusband. He told his friends he cleaned physicians' and dentists' offices and utilised the opportunity to steal medications. However, according to the owner of the company, Kurt's route was largely industrial buildings with little opportunities to take anything. He spent some of his earnings on a rusted old Datsun. One thing was certain about this janitorial service: it left Kurt with little energy to devote to cleaning his own flat, which caused the initial conflict between him and Tracy. Even when he resigned his work, he evidently assumed that he would never have to clean again in his life. His inner artistic life was blossoming in Olympia in ways it had never before. Kurt established a regimen that he would follow for the rest of his life while unemployed. He'd get up around noon and have lunch of sorts. His favourite food was Kraft Macaroni & Cheese. His discerning palate had established that when it came to processed cheese and pasta, Kraft had earned its position as the market leader. After eating, he would spend the rest of the day doing one of three things: watching television, which he did nonstop; practising his guitar for hours a day, usually while watching TV; or creating some kind of art project, whether it was a painting, collage, or three-dimensional installation. This last pastime was never formal-he rarely identified as an artist-but he spent hours on it.

He also kept diaries, albeit the inner conversation he preserved was more of a therapeutic obsessive/compulsive device in which he let loose his innermost thoughts than a play-by-play of his day. The writing was inventive and frightening at times. His songs and journal entries merged at times, but they were both fascinated with human body functions: birth, urine, excrement, and sexuality were all things he was knowledgeable about. One brief segment exemplifies the recurring topics that he would return to: *Chef Boyardee is more vicious, stronger, less prone to disease, and more domineering than a male gorilla. He visits me at night. Willfully unlocking the locks and bending the window bars. I'm spending a lot of money on home burglary devices. He approaches me in my bedroom. I was naked, shaved, and oiled. His skin was covered with goose-bumped thick black arm hairs. I was standing in a puddle of pizza oil. Flour barfing. It gets into my lungs. I sneeze. He chuckles. He saddles me. I want to kick his hot-stinkin', macho fucking ass.*

These inner ideas, which were frequently violent, were in stark contrast to Kurt's external surroundings. For the first time in his life, he had a consistent girlfriend who spoiled him and catered to his every desire. Tracy's attentiveness bordered on mothering at times, and in a way, he needed it. He told his pals that she was "the best girlfriend in the world."

They had indicators of home tranquillity as a couple. They'd stroll to the Laundromat together and, when they could afford it, eat take-out pizza from the Fourth Avenue Tavern (they lived next door to another pizza business, but Kurt said it was terrible). Kurt loved to cook, and he usually served Tracy his signature dish, "vanilla chicken," or fettuccine Alfredo. 'He'd eat the kind of stuff that would make other people gain weight, but he never gained any weight," Tracy said. His weight had always been an issue, and he'd write away to advertisements in the backs of magazines for weight-gain powders, but they had no effect. "His hip bones stuck out, and he had knobby knees," Tracy said. "He didn't wear shorts unless it got really hot because he was so self-conscious about how skinny his legs were." Kurt wore long johns, a pair of Levi's, a second pair of Levi's worn over the first pair, a long-sleeved shirt, a T-shirt, and two sweatshirts to the beach. "He wanted to make himself look bigger," Tracy explained.

His music was the one thing in his life that made him feel bigger, and by the summer of 1987, the band was still going strong. They still hadn't decided on a name, going by everything from "Throat Oyster" to "Ted, Ed, Fred," after Greg Hokanson's mother's boyfriend. They played a few parties in early 1987, and in April they even performed on Olympia's college radio station, KAOS. Tracy gave Jim May at Tacoma's Community World Theater (CWT) a cassette of the radio show and asked him to book them. Tracy and Shelli made invaluable contributions to the band in their early days, serving as press agents, managers, bookers, and merchandise dealers in addition to their primary duties of feeding, dressing, and rehearsing their men.

May provided the band their first non-party engagement, which they performed under the name Skid Row-Kurt was unaware that a lite-metal band from New York had the same name at the time. It didn't matter; they'd change names for every early show, like a socialite trying on hats. This concert, however not long after the Raymond party, demonstrated the band's rapid growth. Tracy, who was predisposed since she loved the singer, was impressed by how far they'd come: "When they started to play, my mouth dropped open." "I told them, 'These guys were good.'"

They may have sounded wonderful, but they sure looked odd. Kurt had tried to appear glam for this gig. To appear taller, he wore flare pants, a silk Hawaiian shirt, and four-inch platform shoes, as he did at numerous shows this year. Musician John Purkey wandered into the CWT that night and recalled "being blown away." I was really blown away by this person's singing voice. I'd never heard anything like his voice before. It was unmistakable. "One song in particular, 'Love Buzz,' stood out."

"Love Buzz" was one of the band's missing puzzle pieces. Krist discovered the song on an album by a Dutch band called the Shocking Blue, and Kurt quickly embraced it and made it their signature track. It started with a mid-tempo drum beat but gradually became a swirling guitar riff. Their rendition of the song combined psychedelic trance with a thudding, slowed-down intensity from

Krist's bass component. Kurt would perform the guitar solo while lying on his back on the floor.

They started playing at the CWT on a regular basis, however to say they created an audience there would be an exaggeration. The theatre itself was a former pornographic movie house, with the only source of heat being a propane blower that operated noisily even during the band's performances. The "ever-present smell of urine" was mentioned by Kurt. The majority of their early fans came to watch other bands-the night before Kurt played, the lineup included Bleeder, Panic, and Lethal Dose. "Jim May booked those guys when nobody else would touch them," Buzz Osborne explained. "It was where they cut their milk teeth." Kurt, who was continually learning from Buzz, knew that even performing in front of their friends was an opportunity to progress. "I could count on them to play at any time," May recalled. "Kurt would never take any money, which was also good for me because I was only doing about twelve shows a month, and only two would make money." Kurt had properly assessed his situation and decided that playing for free would bring the band additional gigs and experience. What were they looking for in the first place? Tracy and Shelli were there.

Shelli had gotten a job at the Boeing cafeteria alongside Tracy. She and Krist had moved to Tacoma, some 30 miles north of Olympia. The band briefly disbanded as a result of the relocation. Kurt used to take the bus back for rehearsals because Krist and Aaron both lived in the Aberdeen area. But, with Krist in Tacoma and working two jobs (at Sears and as an industrial painter), Kurt seemed to be the only one who had time for the band. He wrote Krist a letter to persuade him to rejoin the organisation. "It was funny; it was almost like a commercial," Krist recalled. "'Come, join the band,' it said. There is no obligation. There is no obligation (well, some).' 'Yeah, let's do it again,' I said when I called him. We constructed a rehearsal space in the basement of our house. We went to construction sites, grabbed scraps, and built it out of old two-by-fours and carpet." Kurt and Krist had known each other for a while, but the second formation of the band would deepen their friendship. Despite the fact that neither was particularly excellent at communicating their emotions, they formed a brotherly tie that appeared deeper than any other relationship in their lives.

Even with a practice space in Tacoma, as 1987 came to a close, they were confronted with the drummer issue, which would torment them for the next four years. Burckhard was still in Grays Harbor, and with a new job as the assistant manager at the Aberdeen Burger King, he couldn't play with them any longer. Kurt responded by placing a "Musicians Wanted" ad in The Rocket's October 1987 issue: "SERIOUS DRUMMER WANTED. Black Flag, Melvins, Zeppelin, Scratch Acid, and Ethel Merman are all examples of underground attitude. As versatile as they come. Kurdt 352-0992." They had no real takers, so by December, Kurt and Krist were practising with Dale Crover, who had returned from California, and talking about recording a demo. During 1987, Kurt had dozens of tunes that he wanted to record. He saw an ad for Reciprocal, a recording studio that paid only $20 per hour, and scheduled a January session with up-and-coming producer Jack Endino. Endino had no idea who Kurt was, so he scribbled "Kurt Covain" in his schedule.

On January 23, 1988, Novoselic's friend drove the band and their gear up to Seattle in a shingle-covered camper heated by a wood stove. It appeared to be a rural shack dumped on a pickup truck, which it was. Driving into town, they resembled the Beverly Hillbillies, with wood smoke billowing from the back of the camper and their truck scraping against road climbs.

Chris Hanszek and Endino ran Reciprocal. Mudhoney, Soundgarden, and Mother Love Bone had all performed there, and by 1988, it had become famous. The studio itself was only 900 square feet, with a control room so small that three people couldn't stand in it at the same time. "The carpets were worn, the door frames all were coming apart and tacked back a few times, and it showed its age," Hanszek said. "You could see that the place had the signs of 10,000 musicians who had rubbed their elbows against the place." Kurt and Krist, on the other hand, were looking for more than just a demo tape; they wanted to be in the same league as these other bands. They skipped the introductions and began recording nearly immediately. They recorded and mixed nine and a half songs in less than six hours. The final song, "Pen Cap Chew," was left unfinished because the reel of tape ran out during the recording and the band didn't want to spend the extra $30 for another tape reel. The band impressed Endino, but not terribly so. Kurt paid the $152.44 bill in cash at the end of the day, money he said he'd saved working as a janitor. The camper was subsequently reloaded with equipment, and the band travelled south-they also had a gig scheduled at Tacoma's Community World Theater that day. They listened to the demos twice during the hour-long trip. The 10 songs were "If You Must," "Downer," "Floyd the Barber," "Paper Cuts," "Spank Thru," "Hairspray Queen," "Aero Zeppelin," "Beeswax," "Mexican Seafood," and the first half of "Pen Cap Chew." When it was time for their set, they played the same ten songs in the same order. Kurt's first day as a "real" musician was filled with achievements. He'd been to a studio in Seattle and performed in front of a twenty-person audience. "They were great," Dave Foster, who was in another band on the bill that night, said of the performance. Crover was a killer, though you couldn't hear him over the propane blower because it was such a cold night."

Backstage, an occurrence occurred that would have far-reaching consequences for Kurt. Crover was a veteran compared to Krist and Kurt, and he and the Melvins had played the CWT several times. Crover asked Kurt how much they were paid for the gig, and when Kurt informed him it was free, he protested. May revealed that he'd tried to compensate the band for their past few gigs-the club was finally doing better-but Kurt refused to take any money. Crover began ranting, and Kurt finally stated, "We're not taking any money." Even if the fee was only $20, Crover maintained, there was a principle at stake: "You should never do this, Kurt. These individuals are taking advantage of you. You're always going to get screwed. You have to get your money." Kurt and Krist, on the other hand, saw the reality of May's condition. May eventually came up with a solution that would allow Kurt to maintain his integrity while also making Crover happy: he got the band to accept $10 for gas. Kurt stuffed the $10 money into his pocket and muttered, "Thanks." He left the club that night as a professional musician for the first time in his life, fingering the bill all the way home.

Kurt turned 21 a month later, finally completing the American rite of passage that allowed him to legally purchase liquor. He and Tracy became drunk and ate pizza, which Kurt paid for. Kurt had an on-again, off-again connection with booze. He was drinking and doing drugs less when he was with Tracy than when he was in the Aberdeen hut. None of his friends recall him being the most inebriated of their group-that honour generally went to Krist or Dylan Carlson, who lived next door to Kurt on Pear Street at the time—and at times Kurt was quite restrained. Matthew "Slim" Moon, their other neighbour, had stopped drinking two years before, so there were models of sobriety about. Kurt's poverty in 1988 meant he could hardly afford food, so a luxury like booze was reserved for special occasions or raiding someone else's fridge.

Kurt had temporarily quit smoking and was adamant about others not smoking near him when he turned 21 (he signed a note to a friend that year as "the stuck-up rock star who bitches about exhaust fumes"). He believed that smoking affected both his singing voice and his health. Kurt was always a curious mix of self-preservation and self-destruction, and if you met him one night, you'd be hard pressed to believe he was the same person two weeks later. "We once went to a party in Tacoma," Tracy said, "and the next morning he was asking me what he did because he was so drunk." And I informed him that he had smoked a cigarette. He was taken aback!"

Kurt's sister Kim came to visit around the time he turned 21, and they bonded like they hadn't in years, remembering their common childhood trauma. "He got me ripped on Long Island Iced Teas at his house," Kim told the story. "I got sick, but it was a fun time." Kurt had quit drinking before gigs by 1988, and his emphasis was always on the band, to the exclusion of everything else. He was as dedicated to music at 21 as he would ever be. He breathed, slept, and lived in the band.

Kurt was certain that getting a video on MTV was their path to stardom even before the band had a name. Kurt persuaded the band to perform at the Aberdeen RadioShack while a friend videotaped the show on a low-budget video camera with several special effects. Kurt, too, noticed that the finished recording looked more like amateurs attempting to be rock stars than professional musicians.

Crover left the band's employ soon after their RadioShack concert to join the Melvins in California. They'd always understood Crover was merely a short-term fix for their drummer problem. The Melvins' departure reflected what many Northwest musicians believed at the time: it had been so long since any Northwest band had broken through—Heart having been the last big success-that moving to a more crowded centre appeared the only way to fame. Losing Crover exacerbated Kurt's unhappiness, but it also helped him develop his own identity, and his group could be considered something other than a Melvins offshoot. As late as mid-1988, Kurt was better known in Olympia as a Melvins roadie than as the leader of his own band.

That would soon alter. Crover had recommended Dave Foster, an Aberdeen drummer who was hard-pounding and hard-living. Though having a drummer back in Grays Harbor remained a logistical challenge, Kurt now had his Datsun to assist. When it was running, which wasn't often, he'd travel to Aberdeen, pick up Foster, bring him to Tacoma for practice, and then reverse the entire route later that night or morning, putting in hours of driving.

Their first show with Foster was a party at the Caddyshack, an Olympia house. One of Olympia's quirks was that every student household in the 1980s had a nickname-the Caddyshack located near a golf course. Kurt's first public performance in Olympia, aside from their radio show on KAOS and the Brown Cow show at Gessco, was part of a hard growth curve. It was a cultural shock to perform in front of a living room full of college students. Kurt dressed the part, wearing a ripped-up jean jacket with a tapestry of "The Last Supper" stitched on the back and a plastic monkey, Chim Chim, from the "Speed Racer" cartoon stuck to the epaulette. Foster was dressed casually in a T-shirt, stone-washed pants, and a moustache. Before the band could even start, a kid with a Mohawk hairdo grabbed the microphone and said, "Drummers from Aberdeen sure look weird." Though the youngster was criticising Foster, the remark hit Kurt as well: he wanted nothing more than to be known as an Olympia sophisticate, not an Aberdeen redneck. Classism would be a battle he would fight his entire life, because no matter how far he moved away from Grays Harbor, he felt labelled as a hillbilly. The majority of the Greens were from big cities, and their prejudice toward those from rural towns contrasted sharply with the liberalism they professed toward diverse races. The Caddyshack gig came almost a year to the day after the Raymond party, and it put Kurt in an unexpected paradigm: his band was too hip for Raymond, but not hip enough in Olympia.

He discussed it with his bandmates, hoping that by dressing more formally, they would be viewed more seriously. Kurt told Foster to reduce his drum equipment from twelve to six parts, and then he began to criticise Foster's appearance: "You've got to get with it,

Dave." Foster angrily replied: "It's not fair to make fun of me as the short-haired guy- I've got a job. We might have green hair and we'd still look like hicks." Despite the fact that he'd say the exact opposite in interviews, Kurt cared very much what people thought of him. If that meant getting rid of his stone-washed jean jacket with the white fleece collar, which presently sat in the closet of his flat, then be it. Foster's dress, other than the moustache, was no different from Kurt's two years before, which may be why Kurt took the criticism so personally. Kurt had realised that punk rock, despite being labelled as a liberated type of music, came with its own social mores and styles and that they were many times more limiting than the traditions they were purportedly in protest against. There was a dress code.

Perhaps in some small attempt to leave behind his past and the associations the band had with Aberdeen, Kurt came up with one final name for the group. Foster first heard about the new name when he saw a flyer at Kurt's house for "Nirvana." "Who's that?" he asked. "That's us," replied Kurt. "It means attainment of perfection." In Buddhism, nirvana is the place reached when one transcends the endless cycle of rebirth and human suffering. By renouncing desire, following the Eightfold Path and through meditation and spiritual practice, worshippers work to achieve nirvana and thus gain release from the pain of life. Kurt considered himself a Buddhist at the time, though his only practice of this faith was having watched a late-night television program.

The band would initially attract notoriety under the name Nirvana in Seattle, a city with a population of 500,000, where Kurt was confident his Last Supper jacket would fit right in. Jack Endino had remixed the January 23 session and given it to a couple of his friends on cassette. One was given to Dawn Anderson, who wrote for The Rocket and maintained the fanzine Backlash; another to Shirley Carlson, a volunteer DJ on KCMU, the University of Washington radio station; and a third to Jonathan Poneman, co-owner of Sub Pop, a Northwest independent record company. Nirvana's future would be influenced by all three cassettes. Anderson loved the cassette enough to write a story about it; Carlson gave "Floyd the Barber" its first playing on KCMU; and Poneman received Kurt's phone number from Endino. Kurt was there with a visiting Dale Crover when he called.

Kurt has been anticipating this conversation his entire life. Later, he would spin these events to imply that popularity occurred without his intervention, although this couldn't be further from the reality. He began dubbing out copies and mailing them to record labels around the country as soon as he received the demo. He wrote long, handwritten letters to every label he could think of; the fact that he hadn't thought of Sub Pop was simply a reflection of the label's terrible standing. Kurt wanted to be on SST or Touch and Go the most. Greg Ginn, one of SST's owners and a member of Black Flag, recalled receiving that early demo cassette in the mail: "My opinion on them was that they were not that original, that they were by-the-numbers alternatives." It wasn't horrible, but it also wasn't spectacular." Despite the fact that Kurt sent dozens of demos to Touch and Go during 1988, even going so far as to call them "The Touch and Go Demos" in his notebook, the tape made such a small impression that no one at the label remembered receiving them.

The tape made an even bigger impression on Poneman, who took it to his colleague Bruce Pavitt at his day job—at the Muzak Corporation, the elevator music firm. The Muzak tape-duplicating room was, paradoxically, the day job of choice for many of Seattle's rock elite, and Poneman auditioned the tape for those in attendance, including Mudhoney's Mark Arm. They didn't like it, with Arm calling it "similar to Skin Yard but not as good." Nonetheless, Poneman was able to book Nirvana at the bottom of a bill at the Vogue, a small Seattle club, for one of the label's weekly "Sub Pop

Sunday" showcases. These $2-cover shows included three bands, but the beer specials were just as appealing as the music. Poneman inquired as to whether Nirvana could perform at the Vogue on the last Sunday of April. Kurt hastily responded, trying not to seem too eager.

The Vogue was a small club on Seattle's First Avenue that was famous for its transsexual bartender. It had previously been a new wave club and, before that, a gay motorcycle bar. The major draw in 1988 was disco night, as well as beer deals like three bottles of "Beer Beer" for three dollars. In this way, the Vogue reflected the broader status of the Seattle club scene at the time, which had few venues for unique bands to perform. In December 1987, Pavitt wrote in The Rocket, "Despite the desperate lack of a good club, Seattle has rarely seen so many bands." The Vogue didn't have as strong a pee odour as the Community World, but it did have a mild vanilla odour, a byproduct of the countless amyl nitrite poppers crushed on the floor during dance night.

Kurt Cobain, on the other hand, couldn't wait to take the stage. The band made sure they were on time for this crucial gig, arriving four hours before showtime, just like senior citizens going to the dentist. They drove aimlessly because they had nothing to do and knew few people in the city. Kurt puked in the parking lot next to the arena before soundcheck. "It was only because he was nervous," Foster recalled. "He wasn't drinking." Because Foster was underage, they had to wait in their van before their call.

When it came time to play, Kurt had become, in Foster's words, "pretty uptight." They were astonished to see an audience as small as their typical CWT shows when they took the stage. "There was hardly anyone there," DJ Shirley Carlson said. "Everyone there knew Tracy or Kurt from parties or had heard the tape." We had no idea who sang."

At best, it was a mediocre performance. "We didn't really fuck up," Foster said, "like, we didn't have to stop in the middle of the song." But it was frightening because we knew it was for a record deal." They began with "Love Buzz," which was rare at the time, and played fourteen songs without an encore. Kurt reasoned that putting their greatest material first would be prudent in case people departed. Some of the audience did leave, and Carlson was one of the few who had anything positive to say about the band, comparing them to Cheap Trick: "I remember thinking that not only could Kurt sing and play guitar, though together not very well, but he had a remarkably Robin Zander-like voice." The majority of Seattle's rock elite believed the band stank. Photographer Charles Peterson was so dissatisfied with the group that he didn't waste any film on them and questioned Poneman about the prudence of signing them.

Kurt, as usual, was perhaps the harshest critic of the band's performance. When photographer Rich Hansen photographed the band after the show, Kurt exclaimed, "We sucked!" "They were very self-critical of their set," Hansen said. "There seemed to be some talk about them missing some chords." I was quite aback by how green they were. They were completely inexperienced."

Hansen's photos from that night shed a lot of light on the group's freak-show appearance. Krist, at six-foot-seven, towers over Kurt and Foster; he sports lengthy sideburns and wavy, medium-length hair. Foster, who stands just five feet five inches tall, reaches for Krist's breast and is dressed in stone-washed trousers, a white T-shirt with a mountain silhouette silkscreen, and a backward baseball cap with a Corona Beer logo. He's staring off into the horizon, possibly recalling that he has to be at work by seven o'clock that morning. Kurt is dressed in pants, a grey hoodie turned inside out, and a dark pullover, and Hansen persuades him to sit on Krist's knee for some frames. His golden hair had grown to three inches below his shoulder length. He bears a remarkable resemblance to some depictions of

Jesus Christ with his five-day beard growth. Kurt's attitude in one of the photographs-a sad and distant stare, as if he were recording this moment in time-is reminiscent of the figure of Christ in Leonardo da Vinci's "The Last Supper."

Kurt talked about the concert as their first big failure on the way home, vowing they'd never be so embarrassed again. It was four a.m. before they arrived at their destinations, and during the long drive, Kurt promised his bandmates and himself that he would practise more, write new songs, and they would no longer suck. But when Poneman called him a few days later and offered to make a record together, Kurt's memories of the show transformed. Kurt wrote a letter to Dale Crover two weeks later, titled "Oh, and our final name is Nirvana." The letter's objective was to both gloat and seek advice. It was one of many letters he drafted but never mailed, and its contents outline the portions of the night he wanted to remember and the parts he wanted to forget or reconstruct to his taste. So, in the last few months, our demo has been copied, taped, and debated around all the Seattle Scene heavyweights. And the Dude, Jonathan Poneman (remember the guy who called me the other day when you were over?) Mr. Big-money inheritance, Bruce Pavitt's right hand man and Sub Pop Records financial investor, landed us a show at the Vogue on a Sub Pop Sunday. It's a big deal. But I suppose the publicity and constant airing on KCMU helped. The number of people that came to JUDGE us, not to get drunk, see some bands, and have a good time, but to simply observe the showcase event. 1 hr. Every Seattle band had a person there simply watching, and we felt like they should have had score cards. So, after the show, Bruce enthusiastically shakes our hands and says, "wow good job, let's do a record," then camera flashes go off and this chick from Backlash says, "gee, can we do an interview?" Sure, why not. And then people tell us, "Good job, you guys are great," and we're expected to be total socialites, meeting people, introducing them, and so on. FUCK, I'M BACK IN HIGH SCHOOL! I'd like to return to Aberdeen. Nah,

Olympia is just as dull, and I'm glad to report I've only visited the Smithfield [Café] maybe 5 times this year. So, as a result of this zoo-event, we've obtained a contract for a 3-song single to be released by the end of August and an EP to be released in September or October. We'll try to persuade them to release an album. Jonathan is now our manager, and he arranges performances for us in Oregon and Vancouver. He is covering all recording and distribution fees, so we no longer have to pay exorbitant phone rates. Dave is doing well in the gym. Sub Pop plans to take a caravan of two or three Seattle bands on tour sometime next year. We'll see what happens. Do you believe it is prudent, based on your previous experiences, to demand receipts for recording, pressing costs? Enough with the records. Except until one night last month when Chris and I were high and watching the late show (a rip-off of Johnny Carson) and Paul Revere and the Raiders were on. They were utterly idiotic! Dancing around with moustaches, pretending to be funny and ridiculous. It really irritated us, so I asked Chris if he had any Paul Revere and the Raiders albums.

Kurt had already begun the process of recounting his own experience in a way that produced a separate persona at this early point of his career. He was in the process of creating his most famous character, the mythological "Kurdt Kobain," when he began to misspell his own name. He'd summon this finely honed phantom whenever he needed to detach himself from his own acts or surroundings. He exaggerated every detail of a show that he admittedly sucked: The gathering was too small to accommodate "a representative from every Seattle band"; the camera flashes were primarily figurative, as Hansen only shot a few shots. Kurt even attempts to depict himself as an unwilling participant in his own success when recounting the Sub Pop honchos approaching him. However, he was a beginner actor at the time, and he confesses that he intended "to talk [Sub Pop] into" releasing a full-length song. It is worth mentioning that, at least in the short term, Kurt's business expectations of Sub Pop were not met.

9:

Too Many Humans

Sub Pop Records debuted in the fall of 1987, with Green River and Soundgarden among their initial releases. Jonathan Poneman, the twenty-eight-year-old co-owner, resembled a younger and more heavy-lidded version of Reuben Kincaid, the manager on "The Partridge Family" TV show, and his promotional schemes sounded straight out of Kincaid's business plan, especially his idea to send out groups in a Sub Pop van. Most bands on the label were wary of him, and he was universally distrusted. He'd started the label with a little inheritance, hoping it'd be the Northwest's answer to Stax or Motown. Thinking small and working within a budget were not among his many skills as a publicist.

Poneman's partner, Bruce Pavitt, was a long-time Northwest scene staple who had relocated to Evergreen. Pavitt befriended several bands in Olympia, founded a journal called Subterranean Pop (eventually shortened to Sub Pop), and began releasing cassette compilations. He stopped publishing the fanzine but authored a well read column in The Rocket between 1983 and 1988, which Kurt studied with the rapt devotion most lads only paid to baseball box scores. Pavitt was Sub Pop's artistic visionary, and he looked the part: with his crazy-man eyes, scared demeanour, and propensity for strange beards, he resembled the insane Russian monk, Grigori Rasputin.

Sub Pop was releasing a few singles and EPs every quarter by 1988, largely by Northwest musicians. These ventures made little commercial sense because the production expenses of a single were nearly as high as those of a full-length album, but they sold for far less. Many of Sub Pop's bands were so inexperienced that they hadn't composed enough material for a full-length album. The label burned through their funds like an Internet startup from the outset, but they had discovered a small market niche: indie singles attracted record-collecting elitists, and in punk music, these connoisseurs were the taste-makers. By giving their label a cachet and creating a uniform design identity for all of their releases, they had musicians clamouring to be on Sub Pop, if only to impress their friends. Kurt, like hundreds of other inept young musicians, had a grandly idealistic idea of what it meant to record for the company.

Kurt's naiveté was immediately dispelled. The band's first face-to-face business encounter with Poneman—at Seattle's Café Roma—was terrible. Krist arrived, swigging from a bottle of alcohol he had hidden beneath the table; Kurt was initially shy, but became enraged when he realised Poneman was offering them significantly less than the band desired. It wasn't so much a matter of money—everyone understood there wasn't much of it—as it was of Kurt's desire to relaunch the band by releasing a flood of LPs, EPs, and singles. Poneman proposed they start with a single of "Love Buzz" and work their way up from there. Kurt admitted that "Love Buzz" was their best live song, but as a songwriter, he felt it was dishonest for a cover to be his first release. Nonetheless, by the meeting's conclusion, all parties agreed that Nirvana would record a single, with Endino producing and Sub Pop covering the recording costs. Kurt saw getting his own single out as the realisation of a dream.

Back in Grays Harbor, events threatened to ruin that fantasy. Dave Foster had the misfortune of beating up the mayor's son not long after the Vogue show. He was imprisoned for two weeks, lost his driver's licence, and had to pay hundreds of dollars in medical bills. It couldn't have happened at a worse time for Nirvana, who were preparing for a recording session, so Kurt decided to terminate Foster. How he handled his departure reveals a lot about how he handled disagreement, which is to say, he didn't. Foster, who was shorter than Kurt but muscled like Popeye, had always made Kurt nervous. Initially, the band brought back Aaron Burckhard, but after he was arrested for DWI in Kurt's car, they advertised for drummers again. When they found one, Kurt wrote to Foster, "A band, in our opinion, needs to practise at least five times a week if the band ever intends to do anything.... Instead of lying to you and saying we're breaking up or letting this go any farther, we have to acknowledge we have a new drummer. Chad is his name, and he can make it to practise every night. Most significantly, we can identify with him. Let's be honest: you come from a completely different culture. And we feel terrible that we don't have the courage to tell you in person, but we don't know how angry you'd be." Kurt apparently lacked the courage to mail the letter, since it went unopened. Foster, of fact, wasn't from a "completely different culture" than Kurt's—he was from the same culture, although one from which Kurt desired to leave. Foster found out he was fired after seeing an ad in The Rocket for a Nirvana gig.

Chad Channing was discovered by Kurt and Krist at a Community World Theater performance. "Kurt was wearing these gigantic high-heel shoes, and wide, blue dazzle flare slacks," recalled Chad. " Kurt and Krist were struck by Chad's massive North drums—the kit was the largest they'd ever seen, dwarfing Chad, who, at five-foot-six and with long hair, already looked like an elf. Rather than asking Chad to join the band, Kurt merely invited the drummer to practices until it was evident he was a member of the group.

After one of those practices, which were now planned above Krist's mother's hair salon in Aberdeen so they could play all night, the Nirvana veterans decided to show their new drummer around town. Chad was from Bainbridge Island and had never been to Aberdeen before joining Nirvana. The tour was shocking, especially in Kurt's childhood neighbourhood. "It felt like I was stepping into the south side of the Bronx," Chad recalled. "I said to myself, 'holy crap.' It was a disaster. It is most likely Washington's poorest neighbourhood. You suddenly have this instant slum."

Chad was even more delighted when they passed the Gothic-style Weatherwax High School. They also showed the drummer the five-story abandoned Finch Building; Kurt claimed to have used acid there as a youngster, but this could be said of many Aberdeen locations. They pointed to Dils Old Second Hand Store, which had a 25-cent album bin next to a twenty-foot chainsaw. They headed to the Poorhouse Tavern for a beverage, where Krist seemed to know everyone. "It was a redneck city," Chad observed. "It was tons of dudes with Skoal behind their lips, and with Skoal caps on and neon pink T-shirts, and vans with mud flaps, and moustaches."

When the two Indians left the tavern, they intended to take Chad to a haunted mansion in the hills above town. Krist directed the van north, into what accounts for Aberdeen's affluent neighbourhood: a hillside of beautiful Victorian villas built by pioneer lumber barons. However, at the top of the hill, Krist directed the van into the woods, and Kurt began to recount the story of Aberdeen's haunted house, known locally as "the Castle." He claimed that people had gone in and never returned; one room had blood-splattered photos of clowns on the walls. The hillside grew heavily forested as he spoke, with trees overhanging the tiny road.

Krist pulled into the driveway of the Castle, turned off the lights, but left the engine running. In front of them was a structure that had once been a three-story house but had collapsed on itself due to degradation. The roof was covered with moss, the porch had collapsed in, and entire rooms appeared to have been eaten away by little flames. It looked like the remnants of a crumbling castle in some remote Transylvanian countryside in the darkness, hidden by tree limbs.

Chad wondered why neither Krist nor Kurt moved to get out of the van while it idled. They just sat there, staring at the home as if it were a ghost. "Do you really want to go in?" Kurt finally asked Krist. "Nah, fuck it," Krist answered. I'm not going inside."

As Chad later said, he encouraged them to go in since Kurt's stories had piqued his interest: "I was all excited to check it out and see what was so scary." When we arrived, they were just sitting in the driveway, staring at the home, unable to move." Chad mistook it for a dare, part of an elaborate hazing ritual to test his bravery. He had resolved that no matter how terrifying the home was-and it was quite frightening-he would not be afraid to enter. But when he glanced at Kurt, he saw genuine terror. "Well, people have died in there," Kurt said. Kurt had told such persuasive accounts of the terror in the fifteen minutes it had taken to drive from the tavern to the house that he had begun to believe his own exaggeration. Chad's tour of Aberdeen ended when they turned around and returned to town. Krist accepted Kurt's dualism on face value, but for Chad, the dread on Kurt's face was one of the first signs that the bandleader was more complicated than he appeared.

Kurt was filled with expectation and enthusiasm as the new recording session was arranged for the second week of June. During May, he couldn't stop talking about the forthcoming day, telling everyone he knew and some he didn't, like a new parent overflowing with pride, he'd tell the mailman or the grocery store clerk. The band played a few performances with Chad that month, including a return visit to the Vogue and a party at the "Witch House" for Olympia musician Gilly Hanner. Hanner celebrated his 21st birthday on May 14, 1988, and a buddy invited them as entertainment. "They were nothing like any other Evergreen band," she recalled. "You were hit by their sound. 'I've heard this before,' you'd think, but you haven't. It was more rock 'n' roll than most music of the time, with no noodling." Kurt joined Gilly at the party to sing a version of Scratch Acid's "The Greatest Gift," then Kurt played "Love Buzz" on his back on the floor. At the time, "Love Buzz" was the greatest part of their gigs since Kurt was still trying to find his own sound that was raw enough to appeal to his punk sensibilities while still displaying his more sophisticated lyrics. Far too often, the band's gigs devolved into loud feedback sessions, with almost no of Kurt's comments being audible over the din.

While Kurt's anticipation for the single grew, Sub Pop's financial woes threatened to derail the production. Kurt picked up the phone one May afternoon, only to hear Pavitt ask for $200. It was so ridiculous that it didn't irritate Kurt, but it did irritate Krist, Chad, and Tracy. "We were shocked," Chad recalled. "At that point we began to have our suspicions about those guys." Kurt would have been even more furious if he had realised Sub Pop was reconsidering the band's creative direction. Poneman booked a gig at the Central Tavern on June 5, a Sunday night, since the label wanted another look. Jan Gregor, who booked the club, placed Nirvana in the middle of a three-band bill. Poneman called Gregor the night before the performance and requested whether Nirvana could be moved down in the lineup and perform first. Poneman's reasoning: "It's a Sunday night-we don't want to stay out that late." There were six individuals in the audience when the band took the stage. "Bruce and Jon were at the front of the stage, shaking their heads up and down," said Chris Knab of KCMU. They must have seen something that no one else did, because I thought they were terrible." This gig, like many others that followed, was beset by sound problems, which put Kurt in a terrible mood and jeopardised his performance. Poneman and Pavitt agreed to release the track despite the poor sound and weak live show.

10:

Illegal to Rock 'N' Roll

Kurt wrote to his mother the day before his 22nd birthday, saying, "It's a rainy Sunday afternoon and, as usual, there's not much to do, so I thought I'd write a little letter." Actually, because every day has been rainy and slow, I've been writing a lot recently. It's better than nothing, I suppose. I either write a song or a letter, and I'm tired of writing songs right now. Well, it's my 22nd birthday tomorrow (and I still can't spell)." He didn't finish the letter, and he didn't mail the fragment.

Despite the letter's expression of boredom, Kurt's inner artistic life was flourishing. His 22nd year would be nearly entirely committed to creation, whether it be music or painting. He had long given up hopes of being a commercial artist, yet this freedom allowed his creativity to evolve unhindered. He didn't have a job for the majority of 1989, unless you count running Nirvana as a job. Tracy had become his benefactor, a role she would play for the majority of their time together.

Walking into his flat on any given afternoon in 1989, you were just as likely to see him holding a paintbrush as a guitar. But he wasn't so much a painter as he was a creator. He used any tool he had available as a brush and whatever flat thing he could find as canvas. He couldn't afford canvas or even decent paper, so he created several of his works on the backs of old board games he discovered in thrift stores. Instead of paint, which he rarely used, he utilised pencil, pen, charcoal, magic marker, spray paint, and even blood on occasion. Amy Moon, a neighbour, dropped by one day only to be greeted at the door by Kurt, who was sporting the grin of a crazy scientist who had just given birth to his first creation. He had just finished a painting, he told her, this time using acrylic paint, but with one particular addition, "my secret ingredient." He told Amy he added this to every one of his paintings as the finishing touch, the fait accompli, after the piece was to his liking. He stated that the secret sauce was his sperm. "My seed is on this painting," he explained. "Look at how gleaming it is!"" He made a gesture. Amy didn't dare to inquire how Kurt applied his "seed," but she did notice that there was no brush or palette in the area.

Amy hired Kurt to create a picture for her despite his strange ritual; it was the only commission he ever took. She told him about a dream and requested him to draw it. He accepted the project, and she paid $10 for supplies. Amy couldn't believe Kurt had made the picture from her description because it was so reminiscent of her dream. "It's the middle of the night," Amy explained, "and an eerie force is at work." There are no well-defined trees in the backdrop, only shadows. A car's headlights and a freshly hit deer may be seen in the foreground. The animal's breath is visible, as is the heat radiating from its body. In the foreground, an extremely emaciated female figure is consuming the flesh of an animal that is most likely not yet dead. His picture depicts the dream exactly as I saw it."

Kurt's designs were mostly unpleasant, sometimes shockingly so. Many were topics he'd studied in high school art class, but they had a darker tinge today. He continued to paint aliens and exploding guitars, but his sketchbook also had Dal-esque landscapes with melting clocks, obscene body parts on animals with no heads, and pictures of severed limbs. Throughout 1989, his art began to take on three-dimensional aspects. Every week, he went thrifting in Olympia, and anything cheap and unusual was bound to end up in one of his creations. He painted an image of Batman on the back of an Iron Butterfly CD, attached a naked Barbie doll with a noose around her neck, and gave it to Tracy as a birthday present. He started collecting dolls, vehicle models, lunchboxes, old board games (some of which he saved intact, such as his favourite Evel Knievel game), toy action figures, and other random stuff he acquired on the cheap. These artefacts could be melted in the garden during a BBQ or pasted to the back of a board game rather than being treasured or stored on a shelf. Tracy complained that she couldn't turn around without being stared at by a doll. The entire flat came to resemble a roadside kitsch museum, but one that was always under construction and being demolished. "He had this clutter thing," Krist recalled. "His entire house was cluttered, and there was stuff everywhere." He was, nevertheless, a serious artist, and that was one of the ways he expressed himself; it was how he filtered the world. It poured out in a variety of ways, some of which were horrific and twisted. In reality, the entire body of work is decadent and perverse. His theme remained quite consistent. Everything was just messed up and black."

Kurt's favourite plot twist was swapping sexual organs on figures he'd created. Male bodies would have vaginal heads, while female bodies could have penises as well as breasts. One piece from this time period depicts four naked women seated around a gigantic Satan with a massive erect penis. The women's heads are copied from advertising in Good Housekeeping magazine, despite the fact that the image is created in pencil. The figures are linked in a gigantic human chain: one woman is defecating, another has her hand in her vagina, a third has her hand in the next woman's anus, and the final lady has a baby in her womb. All have devil horns, and they are drawn so realistically that they resemble the work of San Francisco artist Coop from the 1990s.

The majority of Kurt's work was never titled, but one piece from this period did receive a meticulously lettered title. It's a stick man with a giant happy face for a head chopping off his left leg with an axe, drawn in black crayon on white twenty-pound bond. The title is "Mr. Sunshine kills himself."

Despite Kurt's complaints about boredom, 1989 was one of the band's busiest years. Nirvana had only performed two dozen performances in its two-year history, under several aliases and with four different drummers (Burckhard, Foster, Crover, and Channing). However, they would play 100 shows in 1989 alone. Kurt's life began to resemble that of a working musician.

In 1989, they embarked on a West Coast journey that took them to San Francisco, where they saw the "Bleach Your Works" sign. They were touring on the basis of a single at the time, which was an unheard-of proposition given the mathematics of their potential fan base; with fewer than a thousand singles sold worldwide, the chance of a crowd in San Jose, for example, having heard of them and liking them enough to go see them was beyond absurd. Some of these early shows drew only a half-dozen people, usually musicians interested in Sub Pop because the label was more appealing than the band. Dylan Carlson joined the tour and recalled Kurt's fury. "It was kind of a fiasco," he admitted. "There were a lot of shows that got cancelled," said the band's manager, "because the band was willing to play for the bartender and doorman." The largest attendance was 400 people when Nirvana opened for Living Color, a more mainstream rock band with a Top 40 song. They were despised by the audience.

If this first tour had a low point, it happened in San Francisco. The band opened for the Melvins at the Covered Wagon, a reunion Kurt had been looking forward to for a long time. But his optimism was dashed when he realised that the Melvins were not as popular in California as they had been in Grays Harbor. They battled to locate gas money, a bed to sleep on, and food to eat, like they had on every other tour date. Tracy had driven down to California with Amy Moon and Joe Preston, friends of the band. The band's entourage consisted of seven folks who couldn't buy a burrito. Someone on the street mentioned a free soup kitchen. "It may have been run by the Hare Krishnas; Kurt was really creeped out by it," she said. While everyone else devoured the free soup, Kurt merely stared dejectedly at his bowl. "He wouldn't eat it," Amy explained. "He eventually got up and left." It depressed him." Hare Krishna food, ten-person crowds asking for gas money, the Melvins as commercial failures, calling up to request your own single—these signified a level of degradation Kurt had not anticipated or planned for. All seven folks slept on a friend's floor in a studio apartment that night.

They returned to Seattle for a more successful gig at the University of Washington on February 25. It was billed as "Four Bands for Four Bucks," and it drew Nirvana's largest attendance to date, approximately 600 people. They were performing alongside the Fluid, Skin Yard, and Girl Trouble, all of whom were more well-known, yet the crowd went berserk during Nirvana's set. In the late 1980s, Seattle audiences began to slam-dance, which entailed a kind of violent, furious twist, usually performed in front of the stage by a whirling mass of teens. When the gathering became large enough, waves of people would collide into each other, as if a hurricane had formed within the audience. Nirvana's frenetic sound was ideal for slam-dancing since they never slowed down and rarely even halted between songs. The ceremonial dance was completed when a fan would ascend onstage and then jump back into the audience, a technique known as stage diving. Kurt sang and played quietly as dozens of kids hopped onstage, only to jump right back off. At points, there were so many youngsters jumping off the platform that Kurt appeared to be in the centre of an aerial training facility for prospective paratroopers. It was orchestrated anarchy, but this was exactly what Kurt had hoped for: to use his music to cause havoc. Many other bands drew a comparable slam-dancing crowd, but few performers could stand in the midst of these stage invasions as casually as Kurt. He gave the idea that he was used to playing as the audience took over the stage, and in Seattle, that was the case.

That day, Kurt gave a brief interview to the Daily, the University of Washington student newspaper, in which he addressed the Northwest scene, calling it "the last wave of rock music," and "the ultimate rehash." Kurt told writer Phil West that the band's music had a "gloomy, vengeful element based on hatred." "In Aberdeen, I hated my best friends with a passion, because they were idiots," he said. "A lot of that hatred is still leaking through," Kurt admitted, but vowed that one day he'd "live off the band." If that didn't happen, he promised, "I'll just retire to Mexico or Yugoslavia with a few hundred dollars, grow potatoes, and learn the history of rock through back issues of Creem."

In the spring of that year, the band welcomed Jason Everman as a second guitarist, bringing them to a four-piece for the first time. Kurt asked Jason to cover guitar parts that he believed were not being done credit as his songs became more complex. Jason had previously played in bands with Chad and had a reputation as a fiery guitarist. He had also ingratiated himself to the band by lending Kurt $600, which was used to pay the Bleach recording fee. There were no strings attached—Everman was, in fact, never repaid—but Kurt listed Jason on the Bleach album cover, despite the fact that he did not play during the sessions.

Nirvana performed at Sub Pop's "Lamefest" on June 9, at Seattle's Moore Theater, with Jason in the lineup. It saw them open for Mudhoney and Tad, two of Sub Pop's biggest acts, and it marked the official release of Bleach. Nirvana took the stage first, and their show was uneventful save for Kurt getting his guitar strings trapped in his hair. Kurt's favourite part of the night was seeing youngsters line up to buy Bleach.

By mid-1989, the Northwest music scene was gaining international recognition, thanks to some astute moves by Pavitt and Poneman, who demonstrated that their true talent was in marketing labels rather than running them. Their decision to name their annual showcase "Lamefest" was a stroke of genius: it immediately disarmed any potential criticism while appealing to disgruntled music lovers who sported "Loser" T-shirts (the label sold as many of these as it did recordings). Despite Sub Pop's financial difficulties, they paid for plane tickets for a few British rock critics to visit Seattle in early 1988. It was money well spent: Sub Pop bands were in English music weeklies within weeks, and bands like Mudhoney were "grunge" movement stars, at least in Britain. The name was intended to characterise loud, distorted punk, but it was quickly used by nearly every band from the Northwest, including Nirvana, who were actually more pop. Kurt despised the word, but the hype machine was in full swing, and the Northwest scene was growing. Despite the fact that there were few venues to play in Seattle, each gig became an event, and the crowds grew dramatically.

Kurt hypothesised in his notebook years later on why the movement exploded when it did: "Lots of flattering press from several occupational English writers... Nirvana was frequently featured in the early wave of 1989 publicity, but in most articles—like one in Melody Maker in March 1989 headed "Seattle: Rock City," they were consigned to a short sidebar as also-rans. Kurt was probably most surprised to hear Everett True's conjecture on what the band would do if they weren't musicians in his first piece of English press: "You're talking about four guys... who, if they weren't doing this, would be working at a grocery, lumber yard, or vehicle repair." Two of the three professions cited were positions Kurt's father had held, while the third was Buzz's old employment.

Bleach played a significant role in Nirvana emerging from the shadow of their contemporaries. It was an erratic album that juxtaposed songs Kurt wrote four years ago with the recent "About a Girl," yet it had flashes of genius. The chord structure was rough on sludgy tracks like "Sifting," yet the actual lyrics—when they could be heard—were sharp and intelligent. When Gillian Gaar reviewed the album for The Rocket, she said, "Nirvana careens from one end of the thrash spectrum to the other, giving a nod towards garage grunge, alternative noise, and hell-raising metal without swearing allegiance to any of them." Kurt expressed similar sentiments in his journal around the time of the release: "My lyrics are a big pile of contradictions." They're split down the middle between extremely genuine ideas and feelings I have, and snarky, hopeful, hilarious rebuttals to tired, bohemian ideals. I want to be serious and enthusiastic, but I also want to have fun and act like a dork."

Kurt properly described Bleach as a mix of genuine and corny sentiment, yet there was enough of both to get it played on disparate college radio stations. The band had put one of Tracy's images on the cover, reproduced as a reverse image in negative, and the effect suited the stark contrast between the dark and pop songs. Kurt's dualism was crucial to the band's success: there were enough different-sounding tunes that stations could play many cuts without tiring out the band. Slowly, songs like "Blew," "School," "Floyd the Barber," and "Love Buzz" became standards on college radio stations around the country.

There was still a long way to go for the band. The ensemble stepped in as a last-minute replacement for Cat Butt for a show in Portland the day after Lamefest. On the van ride down, eighteen-year-old Rob Kader, a fan who had attended every one of their gigs, led the band in joyfully singing "The Brady Bunch" theme tune. When they arrived at the show, however, only twelve individuals had purchased tickets, all of whom were Cat Butt fanatics. Kurt made the last-minute decision to forego a set list, telling Kader, "We're just going to ask you at the end of each song what you want to hear, and then we'll play that." As each song came to a close, Kurt would walk to the edge of the stage and point to Kader, who would shout out the next number. Except for Kader, who was in his element, the rest of the audience was deafeningly silent, except for one Kiss song, "Do You Love Me?", which Nirvana had recently recorded for a covers album and that Kader had sensibly requested.

In late June 1989, the band loaded up Krist's Dodge van for their first major tour, a two-month trek across the United States. Kader and a bunch of buddies bid them farewell. As a farewell gift, Kader sent a 24-pack of Mountain Dew, which is always a band favourite due to the caffeine spike. They had loaded the van with their new band T-shirts, which read: "Nirvana: Fudge Packin', Crack Smokin', Satan Worshipping' Motherfuckers." Krist and Shelli had recently gotten back together, and their goodbye was heartbreaking. Even Kurt was upset about leaving Tracy because it would be the longest they had been apart since they started dating.

Krist had begun to take on more of the booking business, and the van was completely his domain, governed by a strict set of rules. One rule was posted inside the van: "No use of any gas corporation services other than Exxon—no exceptions." To save money, the air conditioning was never put on, and no one was allowed to travel faster than 70 miles per hour. On their first tour, they split driving duties, but Kurt was rarely in the rotation since his bandmates thought he drove too slowly. "He drove like a little old lady," Tracy said. Kurt's persona was full of paradoxes; he could be willing to huff the fumes from the bottom of an Edge Shaving Gel can, but he wasn't likely to be in a car accident.

Their debut gig was in San Francisco, where they played to a small crowd but enough to avoid the soup kitchen. Despite the fact that they were now travelling in support of a record, Sub Pop's distribution was so poor that they rarely found their album for sale. Two days later, when they performed in-store at Rhino Records in Los Angeles, the retailer only had five copies of the record in stock. In L.A. They were interviewed by the fanzine Flipside, and despite the fact that Kurt's name was misspelt as "Kirk" in the printed piece, they felt the tape gave them punk cred. Kurt was asked about drugs in the article: "I kinda reached my end of things to do, as far as acid and pot and stuff," Kurt answered, sounding rather restrained. "I just maxed out on that stuff." You enter the downhill section once you have completed the learning process. I never used drugs to escape; I always used them to learn."

As they travelled east toward the Midwest and Texas, they played to smaller and smaller groups, perhaps as few as a dozen people, largely musicians who would watch any band. "We measured our shows not so much by how many people were there as by what people said," Chad recalled. And a lot of people said they loved us." They were improving as a live act, winning over unfamiliar audiences. They, like the Velvet Underground before them, would soon discover that a thousand musicians outnumber 10,000 casual fans. When possible, they would sleep on the floors of other punk bands they knew, and these personal ties were just as vital in lifting their spirits as the gigs themselves. They stayed with John Robinson of the Fluid in Denver, who had already recognized Kurt's timidity. "Everyone would be in the kitchen eating, happy to have a home-cooked meal," Robinson went on to say. "I'd ask Krist about Kurt. 'Oh, don't worry about him; he's always gone somewhere,' he said. My house wasn't that huge, so I went looking for him and found him in my daughter's room, lights turned off, staring into space."

Kurt bought a big crucifix at a yard sale while driving through Chicago—probably the first religious thing he didn't steal. He'd stick the crucifix out the van window, shake it at passing pedestrians, and then take a picture of their look as he drove away. Kurt carried the cross in his hand whenever he was in the van's passenger seat, as if it were a weapon he may use at any time.

The band slept in the van or camped by the side of the road on several nights, so solitude was rare. They couldn't afford transportation and food, so staying in a motel was out of the question. The only way they could afford gas was to sell enough T-shirts—the "fudge-packin'" shirts rescued the tour. They arrived late one night in Washington, D.C., and parked the van behind a gas station, intending to stay the night. They couldn't sleep in the van because it was too hot, so they all slept outside on what they thought was a piece of grass in a residential neighbourhood. They discovered they had camped on a road median the next morning.

"We usually had the choice of buying food or gas, and we had to choose gas," Jason said. "Most of us did well with it, but Kurt despised it." He appeared to have a weak constitution and was easily ill. And if he got sick, it would make everyone miserable." Kurt's gastrointestinal ailment flared up on the road, maybe due to infrequent eating, and he seemed to develop colds all the time, even in the summer. His health troubles were not the result of a lack of care; in 1989, he was the most health-conscious band member, rarely drinking and refusing to allow his bandmates to smoke near him for fear of losing his singing powers.

When the band arrived in Jamaica Plain, Massachusetts, they stayed with photographer J. J. Gonson with her bandmate Sluggo from Hullabaloo. Kurt played without a guitar at the band's gig that night at Green Street Station because he'd broken his the night before. He was angry over the guitar, he was suffering from stomach discomfort so severe that he drank Strawberry Quik to relieve the inflammation, and he was homesick. After the show, he called Tracy and told her he wanted to return home. The next morning, Gonson snapped a snapshot of the band sleeping on the floor: they shared one mattress, and Kurt and Krist had curled up next to each other like two puppies during the night.

Kurt asked if he could borrow Sluggo's broken guitar from his wall. "The neck isn't even snapped off, so I can fix it," Kurt pointed out. He gave Sluggo an old Mustang guitar in exchange for it, first autographing it, "Yo, Sluggo, thanks for the trade." Throw my a$$ in jail if rock 'n' roll is illegal." He signed it "Nirvana," assuming his own autograph meant nothing.

Kurt later made a new guitar that day. It was pieced together like

Frankenstein just in time for their next gig, which was itself something out of a horror movie. They decided to perform at an MIT fraternity party since it paid more than their club concerts. Kurt lay down on a pool table before the show and kicked his legs like a two-year-old screaming, "I'm not playing! This is ridiculous. We are superior to this. We're wasting our time." His rage abated only when Krist explained that if they didn't obtain the job, they wouldn't have enough gas money to drive home. The band conducted an enthusiastic act, as if to spite the audience, albeit Krist destroyed a sign spelling out the fraternity's name in bones and handed the bones to the audience. Krist was forced to apologise and repair the sign by the brothers. Novoselic was never one to back down from a fight, especially when the odds were stacked against him, but he humbly grabbed the microphone, apologised, and requested the crowd to return the bones. The fraternity crowd enjoyed the show.

The first outward dispute between Kurt and Jason also arose in Massachusetts. Jason had made the mistake of asking a female home after the show, which the rest of the band thought was inappropriate. Kurt and Krist both have rather traditional views on fidelity and groupies. They viewed a musician in a lady band—a wide group that did not include Jason—to be compromised.

In reality, Kurt and Jason had never gotten along because they were too similar in many respects. Both were prone to brooding and spending time alone, and each saw the other's seclusion as a danger. Jason had long, curly hair that he would thrash about as he played, which Kurt said irritated him, despite the fact that he was guilty of the same head movements. Jason, like Foster before him, represented a side of Kurt that the singer didn't want mirrored back at him. Despite the fact that Kurt created all of the songs, he complained about the pressure and never allowed the other members to have much participation. "He didn't want to relinquish any control." "Everyone knew it was 'the Kurt show,'" Chad noted. Kurt wanted

Jason to create some new guitar solos, but when Jason did so, Kurt acted as if he'd overstepped his authority. Rather than discussing it or even cursing at each other, both became morose and unresponsive. Kurt, like in many of his disagreements, converted the professional into the personal, and a blood war erupted.

The band performed at the Pyramid Club in New York as part of the New Music Seminar. It was their most high-profile performance to yet, in front of an industry crowd that included Kurt's idols Sonic Youth. However, the concert was jeopardised when a drunk entered the stage, screamed into the microphone and knocked over the band's equipment. Jason shoved the person offstage and ran into the audience to catch up with him.

Kurt decided to terminate Jason the next day. They were staying at Janet Billig's Alphabet City flat, which was renowned as New York City's punk rock Motel 6. Jason and Chad had gone sightseeing, but Kurt and Krist spent their remaining money on cocaine, breaking Kurt's tour-long abstinence. Kurt determined Jason was leaving the band, but as is characteristic of his non-confrontational personality, he failed to inform anyone other than Krist. He simply informed the other members that the tour was done and they were returning home, and no one questioned him. The band cancelled two weeks' worth of shows, the first time they'd ever cancelled a show. The van ride home was a living nightmare. "No one said a word for the entire drive," Jason recalled. "We drove nonstop, only stopping for gas," they said, completing the nearly 3,000-mile journey from New York to Seattle in less than three days. Kurt never told Jason he was fired; he simply never phoned back.

Kurt and Tracy had a pleasant reunion. He told her he missed her more than he realised, and while he was never one to express himself, Tracy was one of the few people he confided in. That August, Kurt wrote Jesse Reed a letter in which he boasted about his girlfriend: "My girlfriend now has a brand new '88 Toyota Tercel, a microwave, a food processor, a blender, and an espresso machine." "I am a completely pampered, spoiled bum," Kurt thought of the Tercel.

With Kurt's homecoming, a sense of romanticism returned to their relationship, albeit Tracy wasn't happy with Kurt's moodiness after living alone for nearly two months. With Kurt's collecting tendency, she thought they had outgrown the little studio flat. "I'm not staying here in MOULD HELL any longer than the fifteenth," she emailed him in early August. It's fucking nasty." Despite the fact that it was the middle of summer in the Northwest, their apartment had a mould infestation.

It was surprising that anyone noticed mould because, with all their animals, the apartment had taken on the stench of "a vivisection lab," according to Damon Romero. There were turtles, rats, and cats, but the greatest odour came from the rabbit. Stew was a female bunny that was spoiled like an only kid as Kurt and Tracy's surrogate baby. Stew frequently escaped her cage, prompting Kurt or Tracy to post a notice informing visitors that they might be stepping on rabbit poo. Kurt was on the phone with Michelle Vlasimsky, a booker they had hired to help reschedule their cancelled dates, in early August when the phone went silent. Kurt called her back a minute later and explained, "The rabbit unplugged the phone." He joked that his apartment was nicknamed "the Animal Farm." Slim Moon spotted Kurt urgently running his pet cages outside a few weeks later. "I was defrosting the freezer with a knife when I poked a hole in it, and I didn't want the Freon to kill the animals," he said.

They relocated the mobile Cobain museum when a one-bedroom apartment in the same house became available. It was $50 extra per month, but it was larger and located across from the garage, which Kurt had taken over. He used a workbench to repair the guitars he'd already destroyed and to cut more hardwood necks for guitars he hadn't yet shattered. Within a week, the garage was overrun with broken amps, crushed speaker cabinets, and other relics from Nirvana's tour.

Kurt made his first attempt to seek medical care for his stomach condition and weight-gain advice in the middle of August. His malnutrition had become an obsession for him, so much so that he'd purchased numerous treatments from late-night television commercials and tried them all with no success. He saw a specialist at Tacoma's St. Joseph's Medical Center's Eating Disorder Clinic, but no physical cause for his stomach pain could be discovered after rigorous testing. Later that summer, Kurt went to see another doctor, but Tracy caught him at home 10 minutes after his appointment. Kurt's explanation: "They wanted to take some blood, and I hate needles, so I left." Tracy noted he was "terribly afraid of needles." His stomach ailment came and went, and he threw up all night on several occasions. Tracy was convinced it was his diet, which included fatty and fried items despite his doctor's recommendations. Krist and Chad, who were frequently pressing Kurt to eat vegetables, a category he ignored altogether, echoed her concerns at the time. "I won't eat anything green," he declared.

The band went into the Music Source Studio with producer Steve Fisk in the first week of August to record an EP to promote an impending European tour. The two-day sessions found the band recovering from Jason's death, even if their gear was a little worse for wear from touring. "They had those big North drums," Fisk said, "and the kick drum was held together with two rolls of duct tape because it had cracked so many times." "They joked that it was the 'Liberty Bell drum.'"

They recorded five new Kurt Cobain songs: "Been a Son," "Stain," "Even in His Youth," "Polly," and "Token Eastern Song." The quality of these songs constituted a significant step forward in Kurt's development as a composer. Whereas many of his early songs were one-dimensional rants, usually about the state of society, a song like

"Polly" saw Kurt taking a newspaper clipping and building an emotional backstory to go with the headline. The song, originally titled "Hitchhiker," was inspired by a true-life occurrence that occurred in 1987, when a young girl was kidnapped, violently raped, and tortured with a blow torch. Surprisingly, the song is composed by and in the voice of the criminal. Kurt managed to portray the horror of the rape ("let me clip your dirty wings") while also delicately pointing up the attacker's humanity ("she's just as bored as me"). Its literary strength was that it focused on internal dialogue, similar to how Truman Capote developed empathy for the murderers in his book In Cold Blood. The tune, like "About a Girl," is lovely, gentle, and lyrical, almost as if it were planned to catch the audience off guard and result in the listener unintentionally singing a pleasant melody about a horrendous act. Kurt ends the song with a line that could be an epitaph for the rapist, the victim, or himself: "It amazes me, the will of instinct." Years later, upon first seeing Nirvana in concert, Bob Dylan chose "Polly" as Kurt's most courageous song out of the entire Nirvana catalogue, and one that inspired him to remark of Kurt, "The kid has heart."

The other songs recorded during the session were equally outstanding. "Been a Son" is a song about how Don Cobain wishes Kurt's sister had been a male. Both "Even in His Youth" and "Stain" are personal songs about Don that address Kurt's rejection. Kurt writes in "Even in His Youth" on how "Daddy was ashamed he was nothing," whereas in "Stain," Kurt has "bad blood" and is a "stain" on the family. "Token Eastern Song" was the sole throwaway—it's about writer's block and is essentially a single version of the unsent birthday letter he wrote to his mother.

These songs were also Kurt's most intricate musical compositions to date, with fleshed-out and varied riffs. "We want a big rock sound," Kurt said to Fisk, and they got it. When the tape was played back, Kurt exclaimed, "We're in a big studio, and we have a big Top 40 drum sound." To celebrate, the band requested if they might jump on the tables. "It felt like this high, significant in some way, and worthy of celebration," Fisk said. He joined Kurt, Krist, and Chad in jumping up and down for delight as they climbed up on the tables.

Later that August, Kurt formed an offshoot band with Screaming Trees drummer Mark Lanegan, Krist on bass, and the Trees' drummer Mark Pickerel on drums. Kurt and Lanegan had been writing songs with each other for several months, albeit they spent the majority of their time together talking about their mutual love of Leadbelly. The band rehearsed multiple times in Nirvana's Seattle practice area above the Continental Trailways bus terminal. Pickerel recalls, "Our first rehearsal must have been entirely dedicated to Leadbelly." "Both Mark and Kurt brought Leadbelly tapes, and we listened to them on this little boom-box." Kurt and Krist wanted to name the new band "Lithium," but Pickerel proposed "The Jury," which they eventually went with. However, when the group entered the studio on August 20, with Endino producing, the project fell flat. "It was as if both Mark and Kurt had too much respect for each other to tell the other what to do, or even make suggestions for what they should be doing," observed Pickerel. "Neither of them wanted to take on the position of being the decision maker." The two vocalists couldn't even agree on who should sing which song. "Ain't It a Shame," "Gray Goose," and "Where Did You Sleep Last Night?" were subsequently dropped."They were all Leadbelly songs, but they never finished a record." Kurt was sidetracked by another non-Nirvana project: he went to Portland for a studio session with Dylan Carlson's band Earth.

Nirvana then had to return to the road for two weeks of Midwest performances. The audiences were a little larger and more energetic on this trip, much to their surprise. Bleach had begun to receive college radio airplay, and some gigs drew up to 200 fans who appeared to know the songs. They sold a lot of T-shirts and made money for the first time in their history. When they returned to Seattle, they calculated their earnings versus their expenses and came home with several hundred dollars. Kurt was astounded, proudly showing Tracy his earnings as if $300 could compensate for the years of financial support she'd provided him.

Nirvana's first European tour was scheduled for that summer by Sub Pop. Bleach had received rave reviews in the United Kingdom. Kurt had never gone abroad and was confident that the band would be more popular in Europe. He assured Tracy he'd return with thousands of dollars and postcards from every nation he visited.

11:

Candy, Puppies, Love - London, England

Kurt landed in London on the 20th of October, 1989. He had three days off before the first show and wanted to go to the British Museum, but he was sick, so he settled for having his picture shot at the entrance. Kurt stayed in the hotel with bronchitis, a chronic disease, while his bandmates visited the British pubs. Kurt didn't drink or consume pot at the time due to stomach difficulties. He would pound his chest with his fist in an attempt to cure himself, believing that the violence would loosen his phlegm.

Tad, another Sub Pop band lead by Tad Doyle, a 300-pound former butcher from Idaho, was touring Europe with the band. Because the two bands shared a deep and powerful sound, and because Tad was almost freakishly obese, a brilliant U.K. One event was promoted as "Heavier Than Heaven," and the play on words became the official title of the tour, which was used on posters and in newspaper advertisements. The sombre themes of tracks like Nirvana's "Downer" and Tad's "Cyanide Bath" would undoubtedly overwhelm you if the sheer volume did not. In a gesture of brotherhood, they planned to co-headline, switching off as openers.

Kurt had expected fame and money in Europe, but instead found a low-budget tour that required the band to play 37 shows in 42 days in nine different countries, a route that could only be completed if they drove all night. Their Sub Pop-rented vehicle was a downsized ten-seat Fiat van that had to carry their equipment, tour material, three Nirvana members, four Tad members, and two crew members. Given Tad's girth, Krist's height, and Tad's drummer's insistence on standing up in the van, daily loading could take an hour and resembled something out of a Marx Brothers performance. Tad Doyle had to undergo almost ritualistic daily vomiting prior to departure due to several gastrointestinal issues. This last ailment was so consistent that it could have been included into the tour itinerary: "10 a.m., load the van; 10:10, Tad vomits."

Tad's innermost workings enchanted Kurt. He was experiencing stomach cramps, but he merely vomited bile or blood. "Before Tad would get in the van, Kurt would hold this plastic basin," Kurt Danielson recalls of Tad. "He'd stand there patiently, holding this plastic tub, a delightful sparkle in his eyes." He'd look up at Tad, waiting for him to puke, and it'd all come out in a wonderful, colourful flood, and Kurt would catch it all. No one else got to hold the tub; it was Kurt's duty and he loved it." Tad also had frequent bathroom problems, which required trips to the side of the road, much to the surprise of English drivers who passed a 300-pound guy emptying himself in the median strip. Tad's digestive system became Kurt's muse that fall, as he wrote the song "Imodium" about Doyle's diarrhoea medication.

The band's exploration of Hamburg's infamous red-light area and its porno stores continued the subject of elimination. Kurt, who was obsessed with the female derrière, had photographed Tracy's behind on multiple occasions. He found mainstream porn misogynistic, but was enthralled with deviant porn in the same way that an anthropologist seeks out new tribes. He was particularly taken with magazines featuring "shit love," the sexual obsession more formally known as scatophilia. "Kurt was fascinated by anything out of the ordinary: anything anomalous, psychologically strange or unusual, physically or socially strange," Danielson said. "All the better if it involved bodily functions." He'd get high instead of drinking or smoking marijuana by watching the strange idiosyncrasies of humanity unfolding around him." Kurt was too poor to buy any porn, but Tad did buy one magazine featuring Cicciolina, a sex-industry star who gained international attention after being elected to the Italian Parliament. Ciccolina was seen getting out of a limousine while urinating in a man's mouth in one photograph. Tad would bring out the magazine and declare, "the library is open," each morning in the Fiat van, and the coveted journal would be shared about.

These adolescent antics were the sole distractions from a monotonous and dismal daily life. "We went to Paris, but didn't have time to see the Eiffel Tower," Chad said. Kurt claimed that the timetable was designed to physically and psychologically break them. The frantic schedule began to impact their performances: sometimes they did incredibly well (as in Norwich, where a raucous crowd demanded encores), and occasionally it all went apart (as in Berlin, where Kurt broke his guitar six songs into the set). "They were either phenomenal or kind of atrocious," road manager Alex MacLeod recalls. "But even when they were atrocious, there was an energy about them." The majority of the fans were passionate and familiar with Nirvana's songs, and several gigs were sold out—a first for Nirvana. However, because the venues were small, neither band made much money.

They did receive a lot of coverage, which, combined with considerable airplay from prominent DJ John Peel, catapulted Bleach into the UK Top Ten. Charts for independent labels. Nirvana's first magazine cover, back in Seattle on The Rocket, came while they were in Berlin. Kurt informed reporter Nils Bernstein that his current influences were "cutie bands" like Shonen Knife, the Pixies, and his latest and greatest crush, the Vaselines. He also addressed what he saw as Seattle hipsters' prejudice against Nirvana: "I feel like we've been tagged as illiterate redneck cousin-fucking kids who have no idea what is going on at all." That is entirely false."

Kurt suffered from a profound depression despite the fact that he was finally performing in front of enthusiastic audiences. On the few times when they could afford a hotel, he would frequently share a room with Kurt Danielson, and the two would spend the night staring at the ceiling and chatting about what had brought them to the purgatory of a Fiat van. Kurt told fascinating stories about his childhood, the Fat Man, the Aberdeen jail, and Dylan Carlson's bizarre religion, which combined Scientology and Satanism. But the most bizarre things he told were about his own family: Don and Wendy, firearms in the river, and his high-school friends hitting on his mother. Kurt admitted one sleepless night that he wished he was at home. "I've wanted to go home since the first week of this tour," he explained as he lay in his hotel bed. "I suppose I could. If I wanted to, I could go to my mother's right now—she'd allow me. "She'd wire me the money," he said, his voice cracking like if he were delivering a complicated lie. "She'd have me, you know."

Kurt broke down onstage a few days later in Rome. Tad had taken the stage first, energizing the audience with cries of "Fuck the Pope," a favorite of Italian punk rockers. The sold-out crowd was pumped by the time Nirvana took the stage. But issues with the sound system enraged Kurt, and after 40 minutes of performing, he climbed a 30-foot stack of speakers and yelled to the audience, "I'm going to kill myself!""No one in the room knew what to make of this, not even Krist, Chad, or Poneman and Pavitt (who had come over for the gig). Neither did Kurt, who found himself in the middle of a crowd yelling "jump" in terrible English. He was still strumming his guitar while the rest of the band stood there watching, and he seemed unsure what to do next. "He would have broken his neck if he would have jumped, and at some point he realised that," Danielson said. Kurt eventually descended, but his nightmare was far from finished. The promoter reported backstage that a microphone had been broken. Road manager MacLeod was opposing this, indicating that the microphone was still functional—they couldn't afford to repair it. Kurt snatched the microphone, spun it around like Roger Daltry, and smashed it on the floor. "There, it's now broken," he said as he walked away.

He recovered sufficiently to play five more shows in Europe before wrapping up the trip in London for another Lamefest. Kurt went all out for this final concert, bouncing up and down on stage until his knees were bloodied. But, mentally, Kurt's tour ended after Rome. He didn't have another guitarist to dismiss, so he practically fired his label this time. Kurt couldn't resist comparing the conditions in the van to the jet-setting style in which Pavitt and Poneman arrived in Rome. Though Nirvana would remain on Sub Pop for another year, Kurt had already emotionally abandoned his label due to a deteriorating marriage.

Krist and Shelli had announced their engagement by the time Nirvana returned to America in early December, with a wedding planned for New Year's Eve at their Tacoma home. Kurt and Tracy went, despite the fact that the drive from Olympia to Tacoma was one of the worst 30 minutes of their marriage. Tracy couldn't watch Shelli's wedding without bringing up the matter of commitment with Kurt, even though she knew it would be painful. During the European trip, Krist called Shelli frequently; Tracy only received postcards from Kurt, one of which said "I love you" twenty times. But on the trip to Tacoma, the only time he mentioned marriage was to make a joke about her marrying someone else. "I'd still like to have sex with you, because I really like it," he said, thinking he was complimenting her. Kurt spent the majority of the evening on the roof by himself, abnormally inebriated, ringing in the new year.

Kurt and Tracy had celebrated almost three years of marriage that Christmas. Despite his financial difficulties, he had given her The Art of Rock, a $100 coffee-table book, as a present. They appeared to be a close couple on the outside, but something had changed within Kurt, and both he and Tracy were aware of it. When he returned from tours, he took a little longer to warm up to her, and the gap between their part-time and together-time was wearing on her tolerance. She was concerned that she was losing him to the rest of the world.

In some ways, she was. As Nirvana's fortunes improved, the band began to supply him with the self-esteem and financial support that she had previously supplied. Kurt had band-related stuff that needed to be done every day by the beginning of 1990, and Tracy understood not to assess where she ranked in comparison. But, in reality, she was also moving away from him. She was a sensible young lady, and Kurt only got worse and weirder. She wondered where it would all go. That February, he wrote a half-fantasy, half-reality entry in his journal that would have worried any lover: "I am a male age 23 years old and I'm lactating." My breasts have never felt hurting, not even after being subjected to titty twisters by bully classmates. Because I've lost my imagination, I haven't masturbated in months. When I close my eyes, I see my father, tiny girls, German Shepherds, and TV news analysts, but no luscious pouty-lipped naked female sex kittens wincing in ecstasy. "I see lizards and flipper babies," and other writings like it made her concerned about his mental state.

Kurt has never slept well, gnashing his teeth and having recurring nightmares. "Ever since he could remember, he had dreams about people trying to kill him," Tracy said. "In his dreams, he'd be trying to fight people off with a baseball bat, or people with knives coming after him, or vampires." When he awoke, often with tears in his eyes, Tracy would comfort him the way a mother would, holding him in her arms and caressing his hair. She promised him that she would always be there for him and that she would never leave. Despite this, he'd lie there, drenched in perspiration, staring at the ceiling. "He had those dreams all the time," she worried, wondering how he kept himself cool while on tour.

Outwardly, he appeared fine during the day, never mentioning disturbing nightmares and instead giving the impression of someone who exclusively dreamed of the band. Nirvana began the year with a brief studio session in which they recorded the song "Sappy," and they were already talking about a new album by summer during their European tour. For the first time in Kurt's career, he wasn't the lone force pushing for a new release—Sub Pop, the press, college radio, and even a growing fan base were all pleading with him for new material. He was still writing at a breakneck pace, and the songs were getting better all the time. Nikki McClure had moved into the flat next to his, and she could hear him playing his guitar through the walls all the time. She overheard a wonderful melody coming through the heat vent one afternoon that winter; he kept starting and ending the song, as if he were making it up on the spot. That evening, she tuned in to KAOS and heard Kurt perform the song he'd been practising all day live on the air.

On January 19, 1990, Nirvana performed yet another Olympia show that would go down in history, but for different reasons than the others. Nirvana would perform alongside the Melvins and Beat Happening at a grange hall outside of town. Kurt used stage blood to make needle marks on his arms as a costume. He wasn't sure what a junkie looked like, so he overdrew the marks, making him look more like a zombie from an Ed Wood film than a drug user. "He was wearing short sleeves, and both arms from the wrists to the sleeves had these bruises," Reeves said. "It looked like he had a disease." Nonetheless, Kurt's effort at a joke had unexpected consequences: his parody was missed on many in the audience, and suspicions spread that he was, in fact, a junkie. Nonetheless, despite the fact that the Melvins headlined, Nirvana were suddenly more popular than their masters. The Melvins finished their concert with a spectacular cover of Neil Young's "Rockin' in the Free World." Kurt was in the front row, raising his fist with the rest of the audience, but he couldn't help but notice that a third of the audience had left following Nirvana's set.

Something even more unexpected occurred the following night, when the Melvins and Nirvana performed at Tacoma's Legends venue. The show was totally sold out, earning Nirvana a $500 payoff, one of their largest to date. A hundred people were stage diving, causing havoc. Matt Lukin of Mudhoney was one of the most obnoxious, using his backstage access to walk onstage and then leap headlong into the audience. Nirvana's play was interrupted three times due to confrontations between Lukin and the bouncers. "He's our friend," Kurt said to the bouncers, alarmed and embarrassed. By the end of Nirvana's set, which included a portion of Lynyrd Skynyrd's "Sweet Home Alabama," there were five security guards in front of the band. That didn't seem strange to Kurt, but what did was watching Mark Arm of Mudhoney standing stage right, bopping his head back and forth throughout Nirvana's play.

Mark Arm, real name Mark McLaughlin, was the undisputed tastemaker of Seattle punk rock. While Pavitt and Poneman cleverly capitalised on grunge, Arm, with his band Mudhoney and his previous group Green River, basically developed the musical style and coined the term "grunge," writing in a Seattle fanzine in the early 1980s. Arm was intelligent, witty, talented, infamous for his partying, and projected the kind of self-assurance that led people to believe he was headed for stardom. In a nutshell, he was everything an insecure Aberdeen boy imagined he could never be. To have Arm be at your concert and be seen having fun was like having Jacqueline Kennedy Onassis attend your wedding and dance all night. Everyone could see Kurt's admiration for Arm, but it had to be most clear to Buzz Osborne, who was seeing his old charge move on.

Kurt had tried, with limited success, to become friends with Arm. He'd frequently swing by Arm's place in Seattle, where he was terrified by Arm's collection of punk rock singles—the ultimate status symbol in their community. "He obviously idolised Mark," Arm's girlfriend Carrie Montgomery said. "Mark wasn't all that impressed by it, of course." Mudhoney were Sub Pop's priority and the Northwest scene's kings at the moment. A number of large record labels were interested in them, but they chose Sub Pop because of Arm's acquaintance with Pavitt.

Even Mudhoney's camaraderie was put to the test in 1990, when Sub Pop's financial woes threatened to ruin the label and every band on it. Though Tad, Nirvana, and Mudhoney CDs had been regular sellers, they were nowhere near the level required to sustain the huge organisation Pavitt and Poneman had constructed. "Sub Pop actually asked us to borrow half of our first European advance," Mudhoney's Steve Turner recalled. Because the label was insolvent, it offered bands equity in exchange for royalties owing. "We said, 'What's the point of that?'" Matt Lukin recounted. "You're going to be bankrupt in two weeks." It was especially difficult for Lukin to see how badly Sub Pop treated his buddies in Nirvana. "I saw how long Bruce had been promising to put out another record from them, and he kept putting them off," Lukin said. "They got put on the back burner."

Kurt's earnings from touring were quickly depleted. That spring, he resumed his job search, circling ads in the Daily Olympian for tasks such as cleaning apartments and hosing out dog kennels at a vet's; he applied for the latter but was turned down. He and Krist decided to create their own janitorial company, "Pine Tree Janitorial." It was one of Kurt's numerous get-rich-quick schemes, and he even designed a flyer for their new venture including images of Kurt and Krist pushing brooms. According to the advertisement, "we purposely limit our number of commercial offices in order to personally clean while taking our time." Despite placing flyers across Olympia, no client ever used them.

Kurt used his free time creating music and performing while he wasn't running Pine Tree Janitorial. They went in the first week of February for their most successful West Coast tour yet, gathering enormous, passionate crowds in Portland and San Francisco (for a Valentine's Day show described as "hot hunks"). Even in cynical Hollywood, people flocked to Raji's to see their show. "That was the night they beat L.A.," Pleasant Gehman, who booked the accommodation, recalled. "Everyone was in amazement. The club barely had 200 people in it, but I believe there were 400." They stayed with Jennifer Finch of the band L7 in Los Angeles, who described them as "looking like the Great Dane and Poodle act at the circus: Chad was tiny, his hair was down to his ass, and his eyes were feral; Kurt was a bit taller than Chad, but with hair that was stringy and long; and then there's Krist, who is so tall it hurt your neck to look up at him."

Kurt also reconnected with an old friend, Jesse Reed, who was now living outside of San Diego, during the trip. They met at the San Ysidro McDonald's, which was famed for being the site of a brutal shooting and which Kurt insisted on including on their itinerary. Jesse travelled to Tijuana with the band for a gig, and later that night, a few days before Kurt's 23rd birthday, the two longtime pals celebrated by drinking a half gallon of booze and snorting crystal meth. Despite his stomach difficulties, Kurt began drinking again in early 1990, and while he still drank infrequently, when he did, he drank excessively.

Kurt returned to Olympia with only three weeks before embarking on yet another lengthy tour, which would include a stop in Wisconsin to record the sequel to Bleach. Kurt and Tracy attempted to revive their romance, but the pressure was palpable to everyone around them. "They didn't interact much in public anymore," Slim Moon recalled. Tracy wanted to have sex more often than Kurt, Kurt complained to Slim. It was part of their relationship's bonding for her; it was an emotional commitment he couldn't give anymore.

Damon Romero dropped over one night in March, and they rented DVDs, a common activity for a homebody like Kurt. Kurt had chosen Alex Cox's latest film, Straight to Hell, starring Joe Strummer and Elvis Costello. During the film, Romero stated to an actress, "Hey, there's that girl from that band down in Portland." Courtney

Love was being pointed out by Romero. Despite the negative criticism the film received from critics, Kurt appreciated it. "It had just enough kitsch for Kurt to like it," Romero said.

The band snuck into an Evergreen classroom with a few buddies on March 20 to film what Kurt assumed would be his own official video release. Kurt's intention was for the band to perform while snippets from television were projected in the background. "He had hours and hours and hours and hours of this wacky shit," filmmaker Jon Snyder recalls. "He had recorded 'Star Search' with an old Donny and Marie routine, bits of 'Fantasy Island,' and all these insane late-night 'Lee Press-On Nail' commercials." The band played the first song, "School," while Donny and Marie tap-danced behind them. Background pictures for "Big Cheese" originated from a silent film about witches Kurt had sent abroad for, as well as some of Kurt's Super-8 films from his boyhood. "He had broken dolls, dolls on fire, or stuff like in Toy Story where the dolls are all put together wrong," Alex Kostelnik, who ran one of the cameras, recalled. Kurt considered extending the shoot and travelling to Aberdeen to include more video from his boyhood haunts. It, like many of his concepts, was never realised.

They packed up the van and went back on tour a week later. Tracy was sleeping when Kurt left, but she had left a message in his notebook that said, "Goodbye, Kurdt. Have a fantastic tour and recording. Stay strong. I'll be back in seven weeks. "I miss you, Tracy." It was lovely, but even in her love, there was a sense of defeat. Tracy, too, was now spelling his surname as "Kurdt." Kurt was no longer with her.

On April 2, the band debuted "In Bloom" in Chicago. They drove all night after the event to Madison, Wisconsin, home of Smart Studios and producer Butch Vig. They only had a week to finish their album, but Kurt reminded everyone of how many tracks they had completed in five hours for their first demo. Kurt sought to conceal the idea that most of their new songs were still in the works. Nonetheless, they were confident that Vig, who had worked with hundreds of alternative rock bands, could modify their concepts. Vig did impress the band; as a drummer himself, he was able to capture the drum sound Kurt felt was lacking in their previous efforts.

Working quickly, they recorded eight songs, including a cover of the Velvet Underground's "Here She Comes Now," for a compilation album. In just a few days, they recorded five new songs and re-recorded two old ones. Kurt was naturally dissatisfied that they hadn't done more. Five of the tracks they recorded at Smart ended up on the Nevermind album.

Kurt found inspiration for the new songs by delving into the deep depths of his own life and writing about the people around him. "In Bloom" was a thinly disguised depiction of Dylan Carlson, while "Pay to Play" ridiculed the practice of charging bands to perform in clubs. "Breed" was the session's most intricate song: It began with the title "Imodium," referring to Tad's diarrhoea medicine; however, there is little in the version recorded at Smart to connect it with Tad; Kurt instead used the word to represent a running on of the mouth. More intricate than Kurt's early screeds, it finished with the line "she said," hunting the song's captured dialogue, and providing another layer of narrative to parse.

Kurt had come up with an album title: Sheep. The moniker was his private joke on the masses he was persuaded would be buying his next attempt. "Because you want to not; because everyone else is," he wrote in a phoney advertisement for Sheep. The ad read: "May women rule the world. Abort Christ. Assassinate the bigger and lesser of two evils. Steal Sheep. At a store near you. Nirvana. Flowers. Perfume. Candy. Puppies. Love. Generational Solidarity. And Killing Your Parents. Sheep." Around the same time, he wrote out yet another fake biography of the band, one that would prove strangely prophetic, even as it was filled with adolescent jokes. It described the band as "three-time Granny Award Winners, No. 1 on Billbored Top 100 for 36 consecutive weeks in a row. Two times on the cover of Bowling Stoned, hailed as the most original, thought-provoking and important band of our decade by Thyme and Newsweak."

A few hours after finishing their final mixing at Smart, they were back on tour, and Vig sent the masters to Sub Pop, even though the band had grave doubts as to whether they wanted the label to release the session. Two weeks later, in Massachusetts, Kurt called Tracy and a long phone conversation ensued—one they both knew was coming but one she had hoped to postpone or avoid. He told her things weren't working out between them, and that maybe they should no longer live together. It wasn't an out-and-out breakup; honesty wasn't Kurt's way of dealing with conflict. "He thought maybe we should live apart for a while because we needed a bigger place," recalled Tracy. Kurt's suggestion was peppered with "maybes" and tempered with the assurance that "even if we aren't living together, we'll still be going out." But they both knew it was over.

Within the next month Kurt slept with a young woman while on the road. It was the only instance of infidelity his bandmates ever witnessed. As it was, the sex was crummy and Kurt hated himself for having been so weak. He told Tracy about it when he returned; there had been plenty of opportunities for him to have been unfaithful over the years, and the timing of this one infraction suggests he was trying to emotionally distance himself, to give her a reason to hate him, which would make breaking up easier.

As with all Nirvana tours, after about a month on the road, the band-and Kurt-seemed to fall apart. At a show at the Pyramid Club near the end of April, they had another bout of sound problems. Kurt's spirits were lifted when he saw one person among the crowd of New York hipsters who was bouncing away, even during their long tunings; he couldn't believe his eyes when he realised it was Iggy Pop. But his elation lasted only a moment before turning into embarrassment: Kurt was wearing an Iggy Pop T-shirt. Other people might have been able to laugh this coincidence off, but to Kurt, it corroborated the rock idolatry he desperately wanted to hide. He ended the show by demolishing Chad's drum kit.

Chad had to pay close attention to Kurt's moods to discern when he might torpedo himself into the drums. It was both a self-flagellation and an aggressive act-Kurt had grown dissatisfied with Chad's drumming. In Boston, Kurt threw a full pitcher of water at Chad and missed the drummer's ear by inches.

By the time the band arrived back in the Northwest in late May, it almost didn't have to be said that Chad was out of the band. Nothing, of course, had been said. But about two weeks after the tour ended, Channing looked out the window of his Bainbridge Island home, saw the van edging its way up the long driveway, and, like a doomed character in an Ernest Hemingway short story, knew the end was near. He was actually surprised Kurt had even come along—it was a testament to how much Kurt liked Chad, despite how he soon would claim Chad "didn't fit in with the band." Many times they had all three slept in the same bed, with Kurt and Chad flanking Krist so they could share the one blanket. Krist did the talking; Kurt hardly said a word and spent most of the conversation staring at the ground. But even for Chad, it came as a bit of a relief. "I'd spent the last three years with these guys in really close quarters," Chad recalled. "We'd gone through hell together. We'd been in shit together, in little vans, playing for no money. There wasn't any big daddy with the big bucks bailing us out." Kurt hugged Chad good-bye. Chad knew there had been a friendship, but he also realised it was now gone. "I knew that when we said good-bye, I wouldn't see them for a long time."

12:

Love You So Much - Olympia, Washington

Kurt broke up with Tracy the same week he fired Chad. It was also a form of firing, and he handled all such departures horribly. Kurt's injunction to Tracy was that they should not live together; nevertheless, in his sluggishness, he lacked both the money and the ability to move out. And she couldn't afford to move because she'd spent all of her money on paying their expenses. They stayed in the same apartment until July, when she moved to Tacoma. They lived in parallel universes for three months, in the same physical place but miles away emotionally.

Kurt's world was also one of betrayal, for while he had told Tracy about his infidelity in Texas, he had failed to tell her the larger betrayal, that he was in love with another woman. Tobi Vail, a twenty-year-old Olympia musician, became his new object of desire. Kurt had known Tobi for two years, but he hadn't had the opportunity to spend a full evening with her until early 1990. He informed Dylan the next day that he'd met the first woman who made him vomit. He incorporated that experience into the song "Aneurysm," with the lyric, "Love you so much it makes me sick." Though she was three years younger, she was more educated than he was, and he'd sit for hours listening to Tobi and her friend Kathleen Hanna prattle on about sexism and their plans to form a band called Bikini Kill. Tobi had her own journal, and in its pages she developed the name "riot grrrl" to describe the punk feminism of the 1990s. She was mostly a drummer, but she could also play guitar; she had a huge punk rock record collection; and she was Kurt's female equivalent, he imagined. "You've never met a girl who knew so much about music," Slim Moon noted.

Despite their mutual musical interests, Kurt had fallen for someone who could never love him the way Tracy had and, more importantly, who would never need him. Tobi was less concerned with relationships than Kurt; she wasn't searching for a marriage and wasn't about to mother him. "Boyfriends were more like fashion accessories for Tobi," Alice Wheeler observed. Kurt was looking for the kind of family intimacy he had lacked since childhood in a relationship, but Tobi saw the traditional relationship he desired as misogynistic.

Even the term "girlfriend" had a distinct meaning in the Olympia punk music world, where few admitted to being in a relationship. It was as if acting like you were going steady meant conforming to the usual conventions of a culture that everyone had gone to Olympia to escape. "No one dated in Olympia," Dylan noted. Kurt's relationship with Tracy was archaic by these criteria; his union with Tobi would defy such traditional roles.

He was still living with Tracy when he first slept with her, so their relationship had started in secret. Even after Tracy left, their relationship didn't seem to proceed beyond coffeehouse conversations and the odd late-night sex. He incessantly thought about her all the time, and he rarely left the apartment for fear she would call. She rarely called. Their relationship consisted largely of attending concerts, working on the fanzine, and discussing politics. He began to interpret her punk rock beliefs through his own lens, which encouraged him to make lists of what he believed in, what he despised, and what recordings he should listen to. One statement he repeatedly repeated was, "Punk rock is freedom," which he began to emphasise in every interview, without ever articulating what he was seeking freedom from: it became a mantra to resolve every paradox in his life. Tobi thought it sounded fantastic.

Despite their intellectual compatibility, many people in Olympia had no idea they were a pair. "The whole time they were dating," Slim explained, "it was unclear whether they were officially dating." In some ways, his breakup with Tracy was inconvenient for her because it put her on the spot. "I don't think she intended to be with him for a long time," Kurt discovered. Tobi was allergic to cats, so his animal farm was normally off-limits. It was also filthy by this point: once Tracy departed, the entire apartment resembled a garbage dump, with unwashed dishes stacked high, unclean clothes on the floor, and Kurt's maimed dolls peering over the scene with their insane, busted eyes.

Kurt had complained about feminists frightening him a year before. But once Kurt started sleeping with Tobi, riot grrrl feminism became easier to take, and he quickly embraced it as if it were a freshly discovered religion. The same man who read Cicciolina erotica was suddenly using phrases like "misogyny" and discussing oppressive politics. Kurt wrote in his notebook two rock rules that were quotes from Tobi: "1: learn not to play your instrument; 2: don't hurt girls when you dance (or any other time)." The "learn not to play" was one of Calvin Johnson's many teachings, which argued that musicianship was always second to emotion.

Kurt met Tobi while performing with the Go Team, an Olympia band based on Calvin, but then the Olympia music scene was centred on Calvin. Johnson resembled a mischievous Marine recruit with his boyish short hair and penchant for wearing white T-shirts. But when it came to punk music, he had the demeanour, if not the appearance, of a dictator, crafting policies the way a newly minted ruler would construct a constitution. He was the founder of Beat Happening, co-owner of K Records, KAOS DJ, and promoter of local rock concerts. He preached a lo-fi, indie rock attitude and governed Olympia in the same way that Buzz Osborne had ruled Grays Harbor. "Calvin was very non-rock," John Goodmanson recalled. "The joke was that if you had a bass player in your band, you couldn't be on K." Calvin's disciples even had their own name: "Calvinists." Tobi was not only a Calvinist, but she was Johnson's ex-girlfriend.

Kurt's self-esteem was tested at every stage of his relationship with

Tobi. Kurt found it difficult to integrate into the cosmopolitan Seattle culture, but even in tiny Olympia, he felt like a punk rock version of "Jeopardy!"" and that one incorrect response would send him back to Aberdeen. He discovered that as a youngster who grew up wearing Sammy Hagar T-shirts, he had to continually employ his "Kurdt" self as a disguise to shield his true past. In his journal, he admitted, "Everything I do is an overly conscious and neurotic attempt at trying to prove to others that I am at least more intelligent and cool than they think." When asked to name his influences during press interviews in 1990, he listed an entirely different roster of music than he had one year earlier: he'd grown to understand that in the world of punk rock elitism, the more obscure and unpopular a band wa Friends began to notice Kurt's divided self more: when he was around Tobi, he may disparage a band he'd praised for the day before.

That summer, Krist and Kurt were meticulously dubbing tapes of Smart Studios demos, but they weren't submitting them to Touch and Go; instead, they were submitted to Columbia Records and Warner Brothers. Kurt and Krist had committed to signing with a major label after all of their issues with Sub Pop, if only to get respectable distribution. This was anathema to Tobi. She stated that her band would never be signed to a major label. Kurt tempered his major label ambitions by telling interviewers that Nirvana would sign with a major, cash the advance money, break up, and then release a song on K. It was a lovely fantasy, and he had no intention of behaving in such a foolish manner as to risk his opportunity at fame and money, as he had done with so many grand notions that had passed through his mind.

Nirvana had handled themselves since their brief employment of Tam Ohrmund, with Michele Vlasimsky as booker and Krist handling the majority of the financial arrangements. "I was the only member of Nirvana who graduated from high school," she said. Sub

Pop sent the band a new draft contract in May 1990, which was 30 pages long and granted the label numerous clear powers. Kurt was well aware that he did not want to sign this contract. He and Krist approached Soundgarden's recognized manager, Susan Silver. She looked at the contract and said they needed a lawyer.

Silver was somewhat aback by how adamant they were about not wanting to be on Sub Pop. They claimed that Bleach received little advertising and that the label never supplied them with an accounting of how many copies were sold. Even though the band was still without a drummer, Kurt claimed that he wanted a big-money deal on a large label with the weight of a big corporation behind him. In Calvin's court, such a comment was grounds for public hanging, but it was even more out of character for most Seattle bands. It also contradicted what Kurt had declared in the press just three weeks earlier. On April 27, when WOZQ radio station inquired if the band was interested in signing with a large label, he responded, "We don't have any interest in a major label." It would be good to have better distribution, but anything else on major labels is a load of nonsense."

But, in the period since that interview, his divorce with Tracy had taken away his benefactor. He now declared that he wanted a "million-dollar deal," but perhaps in a nod to Tobi, he added that even if Nirvana got their big deal, they would "still tour in a van." Kurt had heard of Peter Paterno, one of the industry's most powerful lawyers, and asked Susan if she could put in a good word for them. "I'm going to Los Angeles tomorrow," she announced. "If you come sometime while I'm there, I'll take you to meet him." Response: "We'll start driving tonight and see you in a couple of days."

They met Silver in Los Angeles two days later. Silver brought them to Don Muller, a well-known agent, and when Paterno was unable to accommodate them, she put them in touch with attorney Alan Mintz. Mintz's specialty was new bands, but even as new artists, "they were definitely among the scruffiest that ever came through the door." Sub

Pop was also talking to lawyers, attempting to use Nirvana's growing reputation to convince a major label to invest in them. Mintz mentioned it to the band, implying that they might be able to acquire the distribution they desired through Sub Pop. Kurt leaned over and firmly stated, "Get me off this label!"" Kurt stated that he wished to sell a large number of recordings. Mintz was impressed by their tape and immediately began working to secure them a deal.

It was not a difficult task. Even by the mid-1990s, Nirvana's reputation as a dynamic live act, as well as the burgeoning success of Bleach on college radio, had piqued the curiosity of "artist and repertoire" agents, label staffers employed to sign bands. Bret Hartman of MCA, who had been discussing their contract with Poneman and Pavitt in early 1990, was the first A&R man to express interest. Hartman felt his enthusiasm wasn't being communicated to the band, so he obtained Kurt's home phone number and began leaving messages on Kurt's answering machine.

When Krist and Kurt returned to Seattle from L.A., they went back into the studio on July 11 to record the single "Sliver," which would be released ahead of another U.K. tour. tour. They had hired Mudhoney's drummer, Dan Peters, for this event, while they were still interviewing drummers. This would be their ultimate quick-and-dirty studio session, recorded in the middle of a Tad album during a dinner break. The title was another Cobain creation that had nothing to do with the lyrics, but this time the name was the only thing obscure about the song: it was plain and a creative breakthrough. Kurt had mined what he knew best for topic matter—his family. Kurt had finally discovered his own voice, which evolved as he wrote about his family, much like Richard Pryor, who suffered in his comic career until he started cracking jokes about growing up in a whorehouse. He had discovered his talent as a writer practically by chance.

"Sliver" is about a youngster who is dropped off with his

grandparents and does not want his parents to leave. He begs his grandmother to take him home, but she refuses. Dinner is mashed potatoes for him. He has difficulty digesting his meat. He gets on his bike and stubs his toe. He attempts to watch TV but falls asleep. "Grandma, take me home / I wanna be alone," the unadorned chorus chanted. The song concludes with the boy waking up in his mother's arms. "It's probably the most straightforward song we've ever recorded," Kurt told Melody Maker. It was also one of the first Nirvana songs to employ contrasting dynamics, which would become a band trademark: the verses were quiet and sluggish, but the chorus was a tremendous wall of sound. Kurt was questioned about its significance after its publication, and he had the nerve to declare it wasn't autobiographical. But no one, especially no one who knew him, believed him: "It was about being a little boy and wanting to be at home with Mom, not wanting to be baby-sat by his grandparents," his sister Kim recounted.

Nirvana went on a short West Coast tour in August, opening for Sonic Youth, with Dale Crover as their temporary drummer. Kurt saw the tour as an opportunity to meet Thurston Moore and Kim Gordon of Sonic Youth, whom he thought to be royalty. When he discovered that they treated him like a peer, his self-esteem increased. The two bands quickly became friends, and best of all, Moore and Gordon offered Nirvana business advice, recommending that they explore their management company, Gold Mountain.

They were in desperate need of assistance. Despite the prestige of the tour, they were underpaid, following Sonic Youth's massive bus in their ridiculous small Dodge van, looking more like starstruck fans than stars themselves. MCA's Bret Hartman and his boss Paul Atkinson went backstage after the band's play in Los Angeles and found Kurt and Krist packing up their gear; they couldn't hire roadies. Atkinson invited the band to tour MCA, but Krist refused because they needed to return for his job. When Krist explained that he needed to go sell T-shirts because they needed petrol money to go out of town, the conversation came to a halt.

When the tour came to the Northwest, the native boys drew more attention than Sonic Youth. They were rising stars in Portland and Seattle, with an increasing number of fans praising them after each event. Sally Barry, who was in an opening band on this tour, noticed that Kurt's personality didn't appear to change with the limelight. "He was the first person I ever saw fling himself into the crowd with his guitar and not give a rat's ass," she said. "With other people, there was a conscious thought to it." But it was instant and honest with Kurt." Almost every act ended with Kurt diving into the audience, or the audience leaping into him. Kurt spared his drummer on this tour because Crover had threatened to pound Kurt to within an inch of his life if his equipment was ruined.

Because Crover had to rejoin the Melvins, Nirvana hired Dan Peters as their new drummer and began arranging a U.K. tour. tour. Even as Peters banged the drums for the band at a September 22 concert, another candidate Kurt and Krist had flown in to audition was in the crowd. The show, which Peters had performed admirably, was his one and only with Nirvana.

Dave Grohl, 21, was the band's new drummer. Grohl, who was born in Virginia, has previously performed with the bands Scream and Dain Bramage. The swapped letters of the latter moniker were likely enough to endear him to Kurt, demonstrating, if nothing else, that Grohl shared his sense of humour. Buzz had connected Grohl with Nirvana, resuming his mentor position, and it may have been the greatest gift he ever bestowed. Kurt and Krist knew they had found their final drummer the moment they practised with Grohl.

Only twenty days later, Dave Grohl was performing his first Nirvana gig, barely knowing the names of the songs, let alone the drum parts. But it didn't matter with Grohl: as Krist and Kurt had discovered, he was a monster behind the kit. Kurt had previously struggled with drummers, his perfectionism deriving from his own time on the drums. Kurt stepped to the drum kit during most soundchecks and hammered out a couple tunes for kicks. However, Grohl was the type of drummer that made Kurt pleased he'd picked up a guitar.

Grohl's debut performance took place at Olympia's North Shore Surf Club. The night included some of Nirvana's greatest technical blunders; an electrical problem caused the power to go out frequently, and the band was forced to turn off half of their amps to avoid more blackouts. The only light came from audience members holding flashlights, giving an eerie effect reminiscent of a low-budget independent film. Grohl proved too powerful for his small kit, hitting the drums so hard that he broke the snare.

A week later, the band went on tour in England to promote the "Sliver" single, which didn't come out until the trip was complete. Nonetheless, they played to adoring crowds, their renown in England being far higher than in the United States at the time. Kurt went to see the Pixies, one of his favourite bands, while in London. He called Pixies manager Ken Goes the next day and asked if he could manage Nirvana. Goes had never met Kurt but agreed to meet him.

When they met in a hotel lobby, Goes discovered Kurt was more interested in discussing the Pixies than marketing his own band. "He wasn't your average fan, like the type we always see outside of stage doors," went on to say. "In fact, he wasn't so much a fan as a band student." He definitely had a great deal of admiration for what they were doing. He talked on and on about it." During their conversation, Charles Thompson, the lead singer of the Pixies, arrived at the hotel, causing a ruckus. Goes offered to introduce Kurt to his idol, but Kurt immediately froze. "I don't think so," Kurt answered, taking a step back. "I, uh, I can't." And with that, Kurt bolted, behaving as if he wasn't even worthy to be in the face of such greatness.

Dave Grohl opted to move to the Pear Street apartment after Nirvana returned from England, where he had been staying with Krist and Shelli. The following week, MCA sent Kurt and Krist tickets to Los Angeles to explore their offices. The label wasn't the band's first choice—it had been so long since MCA had a hit that many joked that the band's name stood for Music Cemetery of America—but they couldn't pass up a free ticket. The label booked them a room at the Sheraton Universal Hotel, and when they arrived, Bret Hartman went to see if the accommodations were sufficient. He discovered the mini-fridge ajar, as well as Kurt and Krist sitting on the floor, surrounded by little bottles of vodka. "Who put this in our room?"" Kurt inquired. Kurt had never seen an honour bar despite the fact that the band had toured the United States five times and Europe twice. Kurt stared at Hartman incredulously when he told that he could have everything in the fridge and MCA would pay. "I realised," Hartman said, "that perhaps these guys weren't as experienced as I thought they were."

They didn't know what honour bars were, but they realised they were being taken advantage of the next day when they toured MCA. Hartman and Atkinson had distributed copies of Bleach as well as a note urging the workers to be welcoming and cordial. When they led the band around the building, it appeared that every bigwig was having lunch. Angee Jenkins, who oversaw the PR department, chatted briefly with them and supported them, as did the boys in the mailroom, who were among the few MCA employees who had listened to Bleach. The icing on the cake came when the group was wheeled into Richard Palmese's office, where he briefly shook hands with them before mumbling, "It's really great to meet you guys." I enjoy your music, but I have a lunch appointment in five minutes. "I'm going to have to excuse myself." Kurt wasn't even sure who he was meeting, so he turned to Atkinson and asked, "Who is that guy?""That's the president of MCA," Atkinson said, grimacing. MCA was so eliminated from contention. While in Los Angeles,

Kurt and Krist met with Sonic Youth, who encouraged them to sign with their label, DGC, which is part of Geffen Records, one of the few labels that had not indicated interest thus far.

Grohl had moved in by the time Kurt returned to the Northwest, and his presence momentarily brightened Kurt's mood. Kurt's mental health suffered as a result of his seclusion, which peaked during the summer of 1990. He had all the indications of a traumatised child: he stopped talking except when spoken to, and he spent hours every day caressing his wisp of a beard and staring into space. He and Tobi were spending less time together, and when they did, he felt unwilling to take their relationship to the next level. In his journal, he wrote, "The only difference between 'friends who fuck every once in a while' and 'boyfriend/girlfriend' is the official titles given."

Things temporarily improved when Grohl moved in; he was as laidback as Kurt was reclusive. "The house," Nikki McClure said, "became boy-land." Kurt now had someone to hang out with all of the time. It had a husband-and-wife feel to it." Because Kurt was unable to pick up anything, Grohl did things like wash Kurt's clothes for him. Few others could have handled the apartment's state, but Grohl had spent the previous many years on the road. "Dave was raised in a van by wolves," Jennifer Finch explained. He showed Kurt how to make his own tattoos with a needle and India ink. Kurt, on the other hand, went to an Olympia tattoo parlour one day with another friend to get the K Records logo—a "K" inside a shield— imprinted on his arm.

Another attempt to impress Tobi—and Calvin—was the tattoo. Kurt explained the tattoo to anyone who wasn't familiar with K Records by mentioning his love of Vaselines. Surprisingly, the Vaselines were not on K, although being distributed by the label. "Who knows what he was thinking with that tattoo," Dylan Carlson speculated. "I believe he preferred the records K distributed over the records they released." He should have gotten a tattoo that said, 'K Distribution.' "

It would have been a better idea to etch "the Vaselines" on his arm. Kurt had been preaching the band's praises since adding "Molly's Lips" to Nirvana's repertoire. They were Kurt's perfect band. They were childish, amateurish, and unheard of outside of the United Kingdom. is a minor cult in the United States. Kurt began one of his many multi-draft letter-writing campaigns in his notebook soon after hearing the Vaselines, hoping to befriend Eugene Kelly of the band. These letters were always chatty (in one, Kurt mentioned his "ridiculous sleeping schedule where I retire in the wee hours of the morning and successfully avoid any hint of daylight") and inevitably ended with some laudatory comments about the Vaselines' brilliance: "Without trying to be too embarrassingly sappy, I have to say the songs you and Frances have written are some of the most beautiful songs ever."

Kurt's musical tastes were shared by Grohl, but not his fixation with gaining favour with luminaries. He was significantly more interested in girls, and they were in him. He started dating Bikini Kill's Kathleen Hanna- Dave and Kurt would then perform the Olympia version of double dating with Kathleen and Tobi, drinking beer and making lists of the most significant punk rock recordings. The majority of Dave and Kurt's activities were adolescent in nature, but with Tobi and Kathleen around, everyone became more friendly. Kurt became more appealing to Tobi as a result of the circumstance, because hanging out as a gang was less serious than individual dating. "Tobi and Kathleen would literally say, 'Let's go out with Nirvana,'" said next-door neighbour Ian Dickson. Hanna spray-painted "Kurt smells like teen spirit" on Kurt's bedroom wall during a wild night of partying at his place. Kathleen was referring to a deodorant for teenage girls, and by writing this on the wall, she was mocking Kurt about sleeping with her, meaning that he was marked by her scent.

Despite the occasional night of partying, Kurt was lonely and disenchanted-he spent a few evenings, like a bashful Cyrano, covertly observing Tobi's window from the street. Even while labels continued to call, he was feeling less optimistic about his career for the first time in years. Strangely, as he approached signing a contract after years of anticipation, he was overwhelmed with self-doubt. He yearned for the companionship and friendship he'd shared with Tracy. Kurt ultimately admitted to Tracy a few weeks after she moved out that he'd been sleeping with Tobi all along, and Tracy was outraged. "If you'd lie about that, you'd lie about anything," she cried, and a part of him agreed.

He briefly considered purchasing a home in Olympia. He couldn't actually make a purchase until he received an advance check, but he was sure enough that he'd get a good bargain that he paid a fee to get a list of available houses. He travelled about with his Fitz of Depression friend Mikey Nelson, looking at derelict commercial buildings with the intention of constructing a recording studio in the front and living in the back. "He seemed only interested in the houses that looked like businesses," he claimed. "He didn't want to live in a normal house."

But that idea, along with all of his other fantasies for the future, were dashed when Tobi dumped him in the first week of November. He was distraught; he could barely stand up when she delivered him the news. He'd never been dumped before, and he took it personally. He and Tobi had only been dating for around six months. He'd had casual dating, casual sex, and a casual romance, but he hoped that deeper connection was just around the horizon. He reverted to his old tendency of internalising his desertion and self-hatred. He assumed she left him because he didn't deserve her, not because she was young. He felt so sick that when he was helping Slim move a week later, he had to pull over to puke up.

Kurt got more depressed than ever after the separation. He filled an entire notepad with his ranting, much of it violent and upset. He expressed his sadness through literature, music, and artwork, and he wrote songs in response to his pain. Some of them were insane and angry songs, but they represented a new level of his craft because the rage was no longer clichéd and had an authenticity that his earlier work lacked. These new songs were full of fury, remorse, imploring, and complete despair. Kurt would write a half dozen of his most memorable songs in the four months following their breakup, all about Tobi Vail.

The first was "Aneurysm," which he wrote in the hopes of winning her back. But he quickly gave up on it, instead using his songs to express his deep level of hurt, like numerous musicians have done before. One song was originally titled "Formula," but was then renamed "Drain You." "One baby to another said, 'I'm lucky to have met you,'" the lyrics said, paraphrasing Tobi. "It is now my duty to completely drain you," the chorus said, acknowledging her influence over him but also indicting her.

Other songs were inspired by Tobi, some of which were not obviously linked, but all of them were plagued by her ghost. "'Lounge Act' is about Tobi," Krist pointed out. One line in the song refers to Kurt's tattoo: "I'll arrest myself, I'll wear a shield." Another summarises how their relationship was more about learning than love: "We've made a pact to learn from whoever we want without new rules." In an earlier, unrecorded lyric of "Lounge Act," Kurt more directly addressed his former paramour: "I hate you because you are so much like me." Kurt subsequently told Musician's Chris Morris that the song was inspired by "some of my personal experiences, like breaking up with girlfriends and having bad relationships, feeling that death void that the person in the song is feeling-very lonely, sick."

Though he never explicitly stated it, Kurt's most famous song, "Smells Like Teen Spirit," could not have been about anyone else, with the lyrics "She's over-bored and self-assured." "Teen Spirit" was influenced by many things-his anger at his parents, his boredom, his eternal cynicism-yet several individual lines resonate with Tobi's presence. Soon after their breakup, he penned the song, and the first draft featured a phrase that was cut from the final version: "Who will be the king and queen of the outcast teens?"" At one point in his mind, the answer had been Kurt Cobain and Tobi Vail.

His music was the most fruitful component of the breakup, while his writings and artwork indicated a more furious and pathological conclusion. There were dozens of such depictions, as well as pages and pages of stories with tragic endings and disturbing imagery. One drawing depicts an alien having his skin slowly ripped off; another depicts a woman wearing a Ku Klux Klan hat lifting up her skirt and flashing her vagina; another depicts a man stabbing a woman with his penis; and yet another depicts a man and a woman having sex above the caption, "Rape, Rape." The following screed is not out of the ordinary:

When I grow up, I want to be a faggot, nigger, cunt, whore, jew, spic, kraut, wop, sissie, whitey hippie, greedy, money-making, healthy, sweaty, hairy, masculine, kooky new waver, right wing, left wing, chicken wing, chicken shit, ass kickin, dumb fuck, nuclear physicist, Alcoholic Keep them divided, Ghettoize, united we stand, and disregard other people's sensitivities. Kill yourself kill yourself kill kill kill kill kill kill rape rape rape rape rape rape is good, rape is good, rape kill rape greed greed good greed good rape yes kill.

The most of the wrath, however, was directed internally. That fall, if there was one recurring subject in his writing, it was self-hatred. He pictured himself as "bad," "faulty," and "diseased." On one page, he described how he liked kicking elderly women's legs because "these ankles have a plastic bottle full of urine strapped on them and a tube running up into the old worn-out muscled vagina; the yellow stain goes flying everywhere." He then sought out "50-year-old fags who have the same muscle malfunction but in a different cavity....I kick their rubber underwear and He wrote with such force that the pen pierced through the paper. He made no attempt to conceal his stories, instead leaving his journals open about the apartment. Jennifer Finch began dating Grohl, and she realised his agony after reading some of the papers left on the kitchen table. "I was worried about Kurt," she said. "He was just out of control."

His anger for others paled in comparison to the violence he described against himself. Suicide was mentioned several times. In one rant, he described how he may transform himself into "Helen Keller, by puncturing my ears with a knife, then cutting my voice box out." He dreamed about paradise and hell, alternately embracing and rejecting the idea of spirituality as an afterlife escape. "If you want to know what the afterlife feels like," he told me, "then put on a parachute, go up in a plane, shoot a good amount of heroin into your veins, and immediately follow that with a hit of nitrous oxide, then jump or set yourself on fire."

By the second week of November 1990, a new character had emerged in Kurt's diary writing, and this figure would soon appear in practically every image, song, or story. He purposely misspelt its name, thereby giving it a life of its own. He assigned it a female persona, which was odd, but because it became his great love that fell-and even made him puke up, like Tobi-there was some justice in this gender choice. He referred to it as "heroine."

Made in the USA
Monee, IL
20 December 2023

49987128R00089